16.95

NEW TESTAMENT MESSAGE

A Biblical-Theological Commentary

Wilfrid Harrington, O.P. and Donald Senior, C.P.

EDITORS

New Testament Message, Volume 10

1 CORINTHIANS

Jerome Murphy-O'Connor, O.P.

A Michael Glazier Book
THE LITURGICAL PRESS
Collegeville, Minnesota

A Michael Glazier Book published by The Liturgical Press

The Bible text in this publication is from the Revised Standard Version of the Bible, copyrighted 1946, 1952, © 1971, 1973 by the Division of Christian Education of the National Council of the Churches of Christ in the U.S.A., and used by permission.

Library of Congress Catalog Card Number: 79-53891
ISBN 0-8146-5133-X

4   5   6   7   8   9

Contents

Editors' Preface   vii
Introduction   ix
The Beginning. 1: 1-9   1

PART I. DIVISIONS IN THE COMMUNITY.
    1:10-4:21   7

PART II. THE IMPORTANCE OF THE BODY.
    5-6   37

PART III. RESPONSES TO CORINTHIAN
    QUESTIONS   7-14   55

PART IV. THE RESURRECTION
    15:1-58   135

PART V. LAST WORDS.
    16:1-24   153

For Further Reading   161

EDITORS' PREFACE

New Testament Message is a commentary series designed to bring the best of biblical scholarship to a wide audience. Anyone who is sensitive to the mood of the church today is aware of a deep craving for the Word of God. This interest in reading and praying the scriptures is not confined to a religious elite. The desire to strengthen one's faith and to mature in prayer has brought Christians of all types and all ages to discover the beauty of the biblical message. Our age has also been heir to an avalanche of biblical scholarship. Recent archaeological finds, new manuscript evidence, and the increasing volume of specialized studies on the Bible have made possible a much more profound penetration of the biblical message. But the flood of information and its technical nature keeps much of this scholarship out of the hands of the Christian who is eager to learn but is not a specialist. *New Testament Message* is a response to this need.

The subtitle of the series is significant: "A Biblical-Theological Commentary." Each volume in the series, while drawing on up-to-date scholarship, concentrates on bringing to the fore in understandable terms the specific message of each biblical author. The essay-format (rather than a word-by-word commentary) helps the reader savor the beauty and power of the biblical message and, at the same time, understand the sensitive task of responsible biblical interpretation.

A distinctive feature of the series is the amount of space given to the "neglected" New Testament writings, such as Colossians, James, Jude, the Pastoral Letters, the Letters of Peter and John. These briefer biblical books make a significant but often overlooked contribution to the richness of the New Testament. By assigning larger than normal coverage to these books, the series hopes to give these parts of Scripture the attention they deserve.

Because *New Testament Message* is aimed at the entire English speaking world, it is a collaborative effort of international proportions. The twenty-two contributors represent biblical scholarship in North America, Ireland, Britain and Australia. Each of the contributors is a recognized expert in his or her field, has published widely, and has been chosen because of a proven ability to communicate at a popular level. And, while all of the contributors are Roman Catholic, their work is addressed to the Christian community as a whole. The New Testament is the patrimony of all Christians. It is the hope of all concerned with this series that it will bring a fuller appreciation of God's saving Word to his people.

Wilfrid Harrington, O.P.
Donald Senior, C.P.

INTRODUCTION

CONCEITED, stubborn, over-sensitive, argumentative, infantile, pushy. All these adjectives have their place in a description of the Corinthian Christians for whom Paul was responsible. They were the most exasperating community that he had to deal with, for they displayed a positive genius for misunderstanding him. Virtually every statement he made took root in their minds in a slightly distorted form, and from this defective seed came some of the most weird and wonderful ideas ever to dismay a preacher. With very little experience the Corinthians devised and justified (to their own satisfaction, if not that of Paul) a number of highly recreative heresies. From their fertile minds sprang webs of sophistry that challenged Paul's subtle spirit. Who were these people who, if they tried Paul's patience to the utmost, also forced him to clarify the ideas which have become part of the foundations of christian theology?

The Composition of the Community.

It is commonly assumed that the members of the church were predominantly converts from paganism, but this needs revision. From the way Paul presents his arguments we are forced to conclude that he was writing to a community in which the majority were familiar with Jewish teaching. Many were certainly of gentile birth (Acts 18:7), but they had either become converts to Judaism or, at least, were sympathetic to its teaching. The most natural interpretation of Acts 18:4 is that the 'Greeks' were part of the synagogue congregation, and the furore before the Roman proconsul Gallio (Acts 18:12-17) becomes much more intelligible if we assume that Paul had succeeded in seducing hard-won

Jewish converts. When Gallio refused to deal with what he considered to be a purely internal matter, the Jews "seized Sosthenes, the ruler of the synagogue, and beat him in front of the tribunal" (Acts 18:17). The violence of this reaction is best explained if Sosthenes were in charge of a synagogue in which the proportion of Paul's converts had risen to the point where Christians were in effective control of the synagogue.

Such converts would have been familiar with the Old Testament, and the traditional body of interpretation associated with it. But they would also have been in touch with the efforts to synthesize the teaching of the bible and hellenistic philosophy. They would have been conversant with a confused and diluted version of the type of speculation associated with the great Alexandrian Jew, Philo. In addition, of course, their minds would have been full of the popular cynico-stoic philosophy of the streets, and of the ethical and religious ideas that governed civic and social life of the city.

It seems safe to assume that all these concepts and theories were only half-assimilated. They were not subordinated in an over-arching synthesis. Many ideas were mutually contradictory but, as with all of us, long familiarity had blunted the sense of unease that such tension is supposed to cause.

It should come as no surprise, then, that when the Corinthians heard the gospel it set up all sorts of different resonances. It is natural to try to understand the unknown by referring it to what is already known, and so information from a wide variety of sources was called upon to try to make sense of the words of the preachers. The situation was made worse by the fact that not all the preachers were saying precisely the same thing. In addition to the blunt, unsophisticated utterances of Paul, the Corinthians were exposed to the suave eloquence of Apollos who manipulated complex notions with a facility that fascinated those whose taste was for suggestive mysteries, and to the legalistic approach of Judaeo-Christians associated with Peter.

In terms of social classes the community was a cross-section of the city. In a highly developed commercial city such as Corinth it has been calculated that the population was made up of one-third free full citizens, one-third freedmen (ex-slaves whose freedom was restricted by commitments to their former owners), and one-third slaves. These distinctions had nothing to do with wealth or education. Many slaves had better opportunities for both than some freemen.

Some of Paul's converts were very comfortably off. The demands of public or religious office meant that they were accessible only to those with private means. Sosthenes (1:1; Acts 18:17) and Crispus (1 Cor 1:14; Acts 18:8) were rulers of synagogues. Erastus (Rom 16:23; 2 Tim 4:20) was treasurer of the city of Corinth, and must have travelled at least as far afield as Rome because he was known to the community there. Gaius (1 Cor 1:14) had a home big enough to accommodate 'the whole church' (Rom 16:23). The Roman Jews Aquila and Prisca had come to Corinth as refugees, but had sufficient means to travel to Ephesus where they hosted the community (1 Cor 16:19) and back to Rome where they did the same thing (Rom 16:3). A number had enough money to indulge in legal proceedings (1 Cor 6:1).

The social standing of this group when brought into conjunction with what they did shows them to be energetic decisive persons. They belonged to the 'establishment' of the city. Yet they had associated themselves with the Jewish synagogue, and then joined an illegal sect. They were independent-minded and were prepared to take risks to get what they wanted. It was good strategy for Paul to focus his attention first on such persons (1 Cor 1:14). Their enthusiasm and drive was just what he needed to get a community started.

Of course, once Paul was out of the way, forceful personalities accustomed to taking the initiative were a potential source of trouble, and this is precisely what happened at Corinth. There was a tendency to question Paul's authority, and to inaugurate theological and ethical projects that gave an aberrant twist to what he had preached. It also seems likely that this group were responsible for the disorder in the eucharistic celebration. One wealthy Christian (or a number in turn) probably invited the church to his home for a supper consisting of bread and wine which through the pronouncement of the words of institution became the Lord's supper. But in addition to this, the host would have invited his equals to a meal appropriate to their standing. These started to eat before the slaves and the poor had finished their work, and so these latter arrived for a mouthful only to find the leisured class sated and drunk (1 Cor 11: 20-22).

This situation shows that there were also 'have-nots' (1 Cor 11:22) in the Corinthian church and Paul's remark that 'not many of you were wise according to worldly standards, not many were powerful, not many were of noble birth' (1 Cor 1:26) indicates that the proportion of upper-class members was low. It is doubtful if any of the Corinthian Christians were strictly in the poverty class. He presumes that all can make a contribution to the collection for the poor of Jerusalem (1 Cor 16:2), and he certainly makes no effort to equalize the distribution of wealth as happened in Jerusalem (Acts 4:32-37). In fact, once the unity of the eucharistic celebration is safeguarded, Paul has no objection to the rich enjoying their quality meals as long as it is out of sight of the poor (1 Cor 11:22)! The community at Corinth was middle-class in more ways than one!

Theology and Ethics at Corinth.

According to 1 Cor 1:12 there were four factions at Corinth who gave their allegiance to Paul, Apollos, Cephas, and Christ. It is natural to think that each of these groups had their own theological stance. In the course of the epistle Paul does bring to light ideas in vogue at Corinth which could be associated with one or the other group, but he never provides enough evidence to make the attribution certain or even highly probable Hence, to try to classify the theological options of the Corinthians in terms of these four groups is equivalent to building on quicksand.

A number of the ideas of which Paul disapproves seem to fit naturally into a coherent pattern which can safely be taken as representing the theological position of part of the community. They thought of themselves as possessing a 'wisdom' which made them 'perfect' and fully 'mature'. They had been raised to a spiritual sphere in which everything material was irrelevant. This conviction was confirmed and intensified by the presence of unusual spiritual gifts. For them Christ was a heavenly saviour whose relation to the human condition was left carefully vague. Their conviction of the irrelevance of everything material left them no opportunity to focus on his humanity. They had to be aware of their own physical nature, but in this case they adopted the position that no corporeal action had any moral value. Hence, in their eyes, everything was permissible. They could sleep with whom they liked, and eat what and where they pleased. They were 'free' and any restriction on their liberty was not to be tolerated. To flout the conventions, then, became a matter of principle. They approved of incest and raised no difficulties when men and women attired themselves in ways which obscured their sexual difference. Naturally, this group denied the resurrection because they could see no point in the restoration of a body.

To say that this was the dominant theological tendency in the Corinthian community would be going too far. This group may simply have been the most energetic and the most vocal. The psychological make-up suggested by the positions they took makes it likely that its leaders at least belonged to the upper-class of the community. It is certain that the opinions of this group did not receive the approval of the whole community, because there is clear evidence of opposition.

This opposition is not as unified as the theological stance outlined above. All our information concerns practical issues which may or may not have been related. Since Paul does not criticize their speculative basis, we are perhaps entitled to assume that he approved it. In opposition to the libertinism of the 'enlightened' some reacted violently against the idea that it was permissible to eat meat which had been offered to idols, and others (?) maintained that all believers should be celibate, even if they had already committed themselves to marriage. Some considered the resurrection to be so important that they even had themselves baptized for the dead.

Paul was a brave man to venture into this swirling ferment of conflicting ideas, and our respect for his mental toughness increases as we encounter the various aspects of the subtle many-pronged campaign he waged to bring the community back on an even keel. By turns, he is calm and explosive, rational and passionate. He counters arrogance with irony, and confronts abstract theorising with the realities of life. He is aware of the games they play and shows that he can do it better. He sincerely tries to salvage any element of truth in the Corinthian options while, at the same time, setting things up in such a fashion that they themselves are led to see the error of their ways. Despite the temptation he is never authoritarian. He is paternal but in a bracing astringent way. This letter is perhaps the greatest example of the true pedagogy of love.

THE BEGINNING.
1:1-9.

GREETING.
1:1-3.

> **1** Paul, called by the will of God to be an apostle of Christ Jesus, and our brother Sos'thenes,
>
> ²To the church of God which is at Corinth, to those sanctified in Christ Jesus, called to be saints together with all those who in every place call on the name of our Lord Jesus Christ, both their Lord and ours:
>
> ³Grace to you and peace from God our Father and the Lord Jesus Christ.

THE INTRODUCTIONS to all the Pauline letters reflect the same basic pattern. Paul, the sender, and any companions who may be with him are mentioned first, then comes the name of the recipient(s), and finally a word of greeting. This pattern is common to all the letters of the period. Brevity was a strict rule, particularly in the self-designation of the writer, and in his first letters Paul respected this convention (1 Thess 1:1; 2 Thess 1:1). Here, however, he underlines that he was "called by the will of God to be an apostle of Christ Jesus." This insistence on what should have been common knowledge can only be explained as a reaction to the situation at Corinth where his authority was questioned. Because he was called by God through Christ (Gal 1:1; Acts 9:1-19), he was the equal of Peter (1:12; 9:5) and superior to Apollos (1:12; Acts 18:24-19:1) whose authority rested on his eloquence. The identity of Sosthenes is not certain. He may be the leading

1

Corinthian Jew mentioned in Acts 18:17, but here he is
called simply 'the brother' because those who are in Christ
are children of the one Father (1:3).

The conventions permitted greater latitude in the
designation of the recipients, and the use Paul made of this
freedom very often permits us to catch a hint of his mood as
he writes. His anger is evident in the cold, abrupt "to the
churches of Galatia" (Gal 1:2), and the cautious adjective
"to the faithful saints" betrays his sadness that some at
Colossae have fallen away (Col 1:2). Here he addresses 'the
church', as he does to all the communities which he founded
(note the difference in Rom 1:7; Col 1:2), with the exception
of the Philippians who were his favourites. The secular term
ekklēsia 'assembly' is given a religious connotation by the
qualification 'of God' but, for reasons that will become
apparent, Paul specifies that this assembly is made up of
"those sanctified in Christ Jesus." The basic idea is that of
separation which is the connotation of the corresponding
Hebrew word. In virtue of a divine 'call' believers have been
'separated' from a world dominated by a false value-system.
'Called to be saints' is not an accurate translation of what
Paul wrote, but it does in fact represent a facet of his
thought since he believed that such separation gave the
believers an opportunity to grow in freedom. They are no
longer dragged down by pressures hostile to authentic
development. The root of all the problems at Corinth was a
misunderstanding regarding christian identity, and in this
address Paul provides a rather subtle reminder of *who* they
are. The privileges they enjoy are not the result of any
exceptional qualities they may possess (1:26-31). They have
been chosen, and this choice implies responsibilities which
the present letter is designed to help them discover.

With the Corinthians Paul associates "all those who are
calling on the name of our Lord Jesus Christ in every place,
theirs and ours". The ambiguity of the last phrase is evident,
and the version of the RSV represents a reasonable solution.
Others also acclaim Jesus as Lord (Rom 10:13; Ps 98:6; Joel

3:5).Paul's point here is to counter the Corinthians' sense of superiority by a reminder that they are not unique. The benefits they enjoy are shared by others. We have here a hint of the idea of a universal church, but Paul never lost himself in abstractions. The idea of the church is concretized in the local community.

The greeting is a stereotyped formula which appears in all Paul's letters. Peace, meaning the state of salvation, is pure gift.

THANKSGIVING.
1:4-9.

> [4] I give thanks to God always for you because of the grace of God which was given you in Christ Jesus, [5] that in every way you were enriched in him with all speech and all knowledge—[6] even as the testimony to Christ was confirmed among you—[7] so that you are not lacking in any spiritual gift, as you wait for the revealing of our Lord Jesus Christ; [8] who will sustain you to the end, guiltless in the day of our Lord Jesus Christ. [9] God is faithful, by whom you were called into the fellowship of his Son, Jesus Christ our Lord.

Paul conforms to the epistolary etiquette of his period by passing from the Greeting to a prayer of Thanksgiving. None appears in Galatians because there Paul had little or nothing to be thankful for. This indication that the thanksgiving is anything but a meaningless formality is confirmed by the fact that in each case it is closely related to the situation of the community addressed.

The grace given by God is mediated through Jesus Christ and is experienced 'in Christ Jesus', i.e. the community of believers. Paul's realism demands that this grace (v. 4) should not be separated from its effects (vv. 5, 7). These 'spiritual gifts' are 'speech of every kind and knowledge of every kind'. The reference is to the charismatic gifts with which Paul will have to deal in detail later (chs. 12-14). The presence of such gifts in the community witnesses to the reality of divine grace. The suggestion that they were richly endowed would have flattered the Corinthians, but in reality Paul was damning them with faint praise. In other letters the motive for thanksgiving is the presence of faith, hope, and charity (1 Thess, 2 Thess, Col), faith (Rom), or partnership in the gospel (Phil). The Corinthians were not remarkable for their love of one another, and their commitment to the authentic Christ left much to be desired. Paul was not prepared to compromise the truth by paying empty compliments.

The exaggerated importance that the Corinthians gave to charisms was but an aspect of their tendency to concentrate on the present (note the emphasis on 'already' in 4:8). Paul has to remind them that the present is rooted in the past and leads to the future. The parenthetical v. 6 underlines how the power of God touched the Corinthians. The genitive in 'the testimony *of* Christ' (correct RSV) is probably both objective ('the testimony concerning Christ') and subjective ('the testimony given by Christ'), because it was Paul who proclaimed Christ at Corinth, but preaching was effective only if Christ himself 'spoke' through the personality of the preacher (Rom 10:14, 17). The passive 'was confirmed' indicates the divine origin of the power which flowed through Christ and his minister (in order to heighten the sense of God's transcendence Jews tended to avoid the active voice when speaking of divine intervention in history). In 9:1-2 Paul will argue from the reality of this power (known by its effect) to the reality of his status as an apostle. The Corinthians cannot be permitted to forget the cost at which the present was bought (6:20).

The incompleteness of the present is highlighted by the reminder that the Corinthians "wait for the revealing of our Lord Jesus Christ" (v. 7), i.e. the day when he will return in glory to consummate his achievement by rewarding fidelity and punishing infidelity (3:13; 4:3-4). Here we have an implicit warning that consistent effort is necessary if the Corinthians are to retain what they have been given (9:24-27). They must be 'blameless, irreproachable' on the day of reckoning. However, even though Christ will appear only in the future, he is active in the present, and they can rely on his aid in the struggle to be other Christs (v. 8). The action of 'confirming, sustaining' attributed to God in v. 6 is here attributed to Christ. God no longer acts directly (as in the OT) but through Christ, and so the 'fidelity' of God (v. 9) is guaranteed by the action of Christ who not only mediates the call but sustains the response.

The goal of the call is "the fellowship of his Son" (v. 9). Elsewhere Paul says that Christians are called to 'peace' (1 Cor 7:15; Col 3:15), to 'freedom' (1 Cor 7:22; Gal 5:13), or to 'sanctification' (1 Thess 4:7). Each of these notions implies the others. They are but different facets of the same reality which here is termed 'fellowship' (*koinōnia*). Christian existence is a shared mode of being because, if it is only through love that we really exist (13:2), others are as necessary to our being as we to theirs. Such reciprocity on the level of being creates the organic unity of the New Man (Gal 3:28; Col 3:10) who is Christ (6:15; 12:12). The 'fellowship of the Son', therefore, is quite different from the friendliness of a club.

Part I.
DIVISIONS IN THE COMMUNITY
1:10-4:21

Divisions in the Community
1:10-4:21

THE MOST DISTINCTIVE note of a christian community should be its organic unity (12:12-27). The mutual exchange of power through love is the basis of a new environment, radically different from the 'world', in which freedom becomes a reality. Thus, when Paul heard that the believers at Corinth were divided into hostile factions, he had to do something about it immediately. Without a genuine community to give them life his words could only produce sterile institutions. Such factions arose because of the immaturity of the Corinthians (3:1; 14:20). They tended to treat their apostles as they did the popular philosophers with whom they were familiar, and to classify their preaching on the basis of the appeal it made to their aesthetic sensibilities. This forced Paul to explain the true nature and power of the gospel, and to define the precise role of the apostles in God's plan of salvation. He does this in great detail because he has to wean the Corinthians from the besetting fault of new converts (and the perennial temptation of believers), i.e. the tendency to understand the structures of christian existence in terms of models drawn from a fallen world. Although he appears to jump from topic to topic, Paul here offers a consistent and compact theology of the apostolate.

RIVAL GROUPS IN THE COMMUNITY.
1:10-17.

> ¹⁰I appeal to you, brethren, by the name of our Lord Jesus Christ, that all of you agree and that there be no dissensions among you, but that you be united in the same mind and the same judgment. ¹¹For it has been reported to me by Chlo'e's people that there is quarreling among you, my brethren. ¹²What I mean is that each one of you says, "I belong to Paul," or "I belong to Apol'los," or "I belong to Cephas," or "I belong to Christ." ¹³Is Christ divided? Was Paul crucified for you? Or were you baptized in the name of Paul? ¹⁴I am thankful that I baptized none of you except Crispus and Ga'ius; ¹⁵lest any one should say that you were baptized in my name. ¹⁶(I did baptize also the household of Steph'anas. Beyond that, I do not know whether I baptized any one else.) ¹⁷For Christ did not send me to baptize but to preach the gospel, and not with eloquent wisdom, lest the cross of Christ be emptied of its power.

Here we discover the reason why Paul insisted on 'fellowship' as the goal of God's call. A community of faith should above all be characterized by unity, and this was emphatically not the situation at Corinth. We know nothing of Chloe, and it is impossible to decide whether she lived in Corinth or in Ephesus. There were important commercial links between the two cities, and some members of her household travelled between them. These brought word to Paul that the community at Corinth was split into different factions (v. 11). All were not of 'the same mind and the same judgment' and, in consequence did not 'agree on what they said' (v. 10). The parties, however, were not just apart from one another, but hostile to one another — "there is quarreling among you" (v. 11). 'Quarreling' was, for Paul, one of the dominant characteristics of man without Christ (Rom 1:29; 2 Cor 12:30; Gal 5:20), and it is easy to detect the sadness with which Paul links it to 'my brothers'. In place of

fraternal unity, "each of of you has his own slogan" (v. 12).
Four slogans are given.

(a) "I belong to Paul": The fact that some members of the
community lined up behind Paul shows that others opposed
him. This was probably the only reason for the formation of
a Paul-party, but the stress that Paul laid on his own
example may also have been a factor (4:17; 11:1).

(b) "I belong to Apollos": A cultivated convert Jew from
Alexandria, Apollos had visited Corinth after Paul's
departure (Acts 18:24-19:1). There is no hint that his
teaching differed from that of Paul (3:6), but his eloquence
would have attracted followers among those who found
Paul a poor speaker (2 Cor 10:10; 11:6). Would-be
sophisticates have always preferred brilliance to bluntness.

(c) "I belong to Cephas": There is no solid evidence that
Peter ever visited Corinth. Those who maintain that he did
base themselves on the prominence given him in 9:5 even
though he was certainly included in the just-mentioned
'other apostles'. This is not conclusive, and it is sufficient to
postulate a visit of Palestinian Jewish converts (2 Cor 10:13)
who presented Peter as 'the rock' on which Christ founded
the church (Mt 16:18) and who may have insisted on the
observance of certain Jewish practices.

(d) "I belong to Christ": Since any believer could say this, it
has been considered Paul's reaction to the three preceding
slogans. This, however, is not convincing because the form
of the statement is that of the other slogans. If Paul had
intended to express his own opinion he would have
introduced some variation in order to avoid confusing his
readers. Paul normally uses 'belonging to Christ' in an
entirely positive sense (1 Cor 3:23; 15:23; Gal 3:29; 5:24), but
there is one exception to this usage, "If anyone is confident
that he is Christ's, let him remind himself that as he is
Christ's, so are we" (2 Cor 10:7), which suggests that there
were some who invoked Christ in order to repudiate Paul.
Their Christ, however, was not that of Paul. They tended to
focus on him as the Lord of Glory (2:8), a supra-human

being to whom they related by 'wisdom'. Such intellectual absorption led them to regard the body as insignificant (6:18), and to claim that no physical action carried any moral implications (6:12; 10:23). Much of Paul's effort in this letter will be devoted to convincing this group that they could not have Christ without community, or freedom without responsibility.

A new paragraph should begin with v. 13 whose first question inaugurates Paul's response. The form of the question "Is Christ divided?" expects an affirmative answer, indicating that Paul is here using 'Christ' as a designation of the Christian community, as he also does in 6:15 and 12:12. The community is 'Christ' insofar as it incarnates the love, power, and wisdom that were his (1:24); the identity is dynamic and functional. Paul could hardly have found a more dramatic way of informing the Corinthians of the extent of their failure. He implies that Christ no longer exists among them. He cannot be the Head if there is in fact no Body.

The fact that Paul makes no mention of the Apollos and Cephas groups may suggest that they were not very significant. He is much more concerned to repudiate the Paul group. The exceptions in vv. 15-16 reveal Paul's tendency to rush into things, but his main point is clear. If he did baptize certain people it was purely by chance, and so should not be interpreted to mean that he had singled them out to occupy privileged positions in the community. Crispus was certainly an early convert (Acts 18:8) and so, probably, was Gaius (Rom 16:23). This explains why Paul baptized them. Once the community was established the function passed to others. Stephanas, who was with Paul when he wrote (16:17), may have brought the letter from Corinth (7:1).

Paul's vocation is to preach (1:1), and the content of his gospel is the cross of Christ. The death of Christ was *the* manifestation of the creative love he incarnated. The gospel embodies the same intrinsic power (v. 18; Rom 1:16), and what is important is that it be presented in such a way that its latent power be released. This is achieved only when the preacher is another Christ "always carrying in the body the dying of Jesus, so that the life of Jesus may be manifested in our bodies" (2 Cor 4:10). Paul refuses any attempt to give power to the gospel by rhetorical skill ('eloquent wisdom'), because to make the cross plausible by means of literary artifices is to rob it of its power.

GOD HAS DIFFERENT STANDARDS.
1:18-31.

[18]For the word of the cross is folly to those who are perishing, but to us who are being saved it is the power of God. [19]For it is written,

"I will destroy the wisdom of the
    wise,
and the cleverness of the clever I
    will thwart."

[20]Where is the wise man? Where is the scribe? Where is the debater of this age? Has not God made foolish the wisdom of the world? [21]For since, in the wisdom of God, the world did not know God through wisdom, it pleased God through the folly of what we preach to save those who believe. [22]For Jews demand signs and Greeks seek wisdom, [23]but we preach Christ crucified, a stumbling block to Jews and folly to Gentiles, [24]but to those who are called, both Jews and Greeks, Christ the power of God and the wisdom of God. [25]For the foolishness of God is wiser than men, and the weakness of God is stronger than men.

[26]For consider your call, brethren; not many of you were wise according to worldly standards, not many were powerful, not many were of noble birth; [27]but God chose what is foolish in the world to shame the wise, God chose what is weak in the world to shame the strong, [28]God chose what is low and despised in the world, even things

that are not, to bring to nothing things that are, [29]so that no human being might boast in the presence of God. [30]He is the source of your life in Christ Jesus, whom God made our wisdom, our righteousness and sanctification and redemption; [31]therefore, as it is written, "Let him who boasts, boast of the Lord."

Any attempt to make the gospel palatable by bringing it into line with the tastes of those to whom it is preached distorts it, because in this case the criterion is made the expectations of *fallen* humanity. In consequence, it loses its power. God is not governed by the standards of the world, and the basic message of this section is that believers must detach themselves from the conventions of judgment to which they have become accustomed if they are to really understand the way in which God relates to humanity.

The wisdom of fallen humanity ('the world', v. 20) is concretized in the desire of the Jews for signs and the quest of the Greeks for wisdom (v. 22). The expectation of miracles can be made to look very religious, but it is in reality born of scepticism. It refuses the risk of trust, and insists on linking commitment to security. The Jews were comfortable with what they had and any excuse would do to avoid acceptance of a new divine intervention in history. The situation of the Gentiles was different. Their quest for wisdom was the construction of a revelation claimed to be divine. Inevitably such a revelation imposed only those demands that the constructors were prepared to accept.

Consequently those confined in the complacency of the present saw the gospel of the cross as 'folly' and 'foolishness' (vv. 18, 21, 23). It was irrational and alien. In order to mock the pretentiousness of the assumption that humanity was entitled to judge God in function of its own egotistical expectations, Paul insists that God just went ahead and did something really foolish (v. 21b), because humanity had refused to accept the insight into the infinity of the mystery of God offered by the wisdom displayed in creation (v. 21a; Rom 1:19-20).

Others, however, reacted differently and accepted Christ. They see him not as foolishness, but as the power and wisdom of God (v. 24). These divine attributes are now integrated into history in the person of Jesus Christ. He *is* 'the wisdom of God' because his person is the adequate presentation of the divine intention for humanity, and so the only valid goal of all human aspirations toward wholeness. Unlike other men he does not reflect what humanity is, but what it can and must become. He does not merely display what authentic humanity is but he enables others to achieve it. His personality radiates a transforming love which shows him to be 'the power of God'.

This power is mediated by a preaching which is confirmed by the existential witness of the personality of the preacher (v. 17). But not all those to whom the preaching is addressed hear a 'call' (v. 24) which really enables them to respond. Paul consistently speaks of 'call' only with respect to those who have accepted Christ. It is a question, therefore, of a special grace given to some but not to others. 2 Thess 2:10 is the only text to mention this grace explicitly. All are offered the grace of 'the love of truth' which is the possibility of openness to reality. For those who accept this grace preaching can become a 'call'. On those who refuse this grace preaching makes no impression, whatever the qualities of the preacher.

This is as far as Paul penetrates into the mystery of the reconciliation of divine initiative and human freedom. There is no hint that he maintained the doctrine of predestination that one finds in the works of Luther or Calvin. V. 18 might give the impression that he did, because he contrasts 'those perishing' with 'those being saved'. This classification, however, is based on reaction to the gospel. Some are seen to be on the way to salvation because they accept. Others are seen to be on the way to destruction because they reject. The use of present participles indicates that neither state is definitive. Those who are now in the process of being saved could be damned (9:27; 10:1-13) whereas those now on the way to destruction could be saved.

In order to illustrate the unexpectedness of God's action and to confirm that he operates according to different standards, Paul adduces the make-up of the Corinthian community (vv. 26-31). It is a simple irrefutable ad hominem argument and typical of Paul's realism. In human experience the wise, powerful, and wealthy are those who effect change in society. One would have expected God to choose them as his instruments. But in order that his power might be recognized, God chose the foolish, the weak, the low and despised to implement his purpose.

This does not mean that the Corinthian community was made up of the dregs of society. Some were well-educated, while others enjoyed the privileges of power and noble birth. His point is that the majority enjoyed none of these advantages. This picture of the social condition of the first Christians is probably representative. The gospel made its greatest impact in the urban middle class.

The most significant of the many contrasts emerges if we confront v. 28 with v. 30. 'The things that are not' is probably a reference to the church because it is a type of community that had not hitherto existed. In and through it those who were nothing in terms of genuinely human existence (13:2) come to be, "From him you *are* in Christ Jesus" (v. 30). Only those who are in Christ exist as God intended them to exist, for only they can love creatively in freedom. Such authentic existence is fundamentally a new perspective on reality. It is the 'wisdom' which is given in Christ (v. 30; contrast vv. 19-20; 27), and this alone permits us to understand exactly what 'righteousness, sanctification, and redemption' involve. We are 'freed' from the world if we are no longer forced to accept its standards and conventions of judgment. By that fact we are 'separated' from the world, and in consequence are capable of becoming what God intended us to be. It is only as righteous before God that man is what he should be. Any sentiment of pride (vv. 29, 31), therefore, is out of place, because it is from God that we receive all that we are and all that we enjoy.

THE POWER OF PAUL'S PREACHING.
2:1-5.

> **2** When I came to you, brethren, I did not come proclaiming to you the testimony of God in lofty words or wisdom. ²For I decided to know nothing among you except Jesus Christ and him crucified. ³And I was with you in weakness and in much fear and trembling: ⁴and my speech and my message were not in plausible words of wisdom, but in demonstration of the Spirit and power. ⁵that your faith might not rest in the wisdom of men but in the power of God.

Paul here emphasises his fidelity to the principle enunciated in the last section by developing more fully the content of v. 17. He had come to Corinth in a depressed state. After his failure at Athens (Acts 17:32-33) he had to face the cynical wickedness of a great port-city. His chronic illness (2 Cor 12:7) may have flared up, and he was aware that his physical presence was not impressive (2 Cor 10:10). Yet he refused the artifices of rhetoric and logic, and simply proclaimed Jesus as the Crucified Lord. The fact that some Corinthians responded to the 'call' which he mediated proved that his words were carried by 'the power of the spirit'. As in v. 18 Paul works from effect to cause. The existence of the community is the evidence of divine power (9:1-2; 2 Cor 3:2-3). There is no reference to miracles. The faith of the Corinthians, therefore, is rooted in the power of God, and is not inspired by the persuasive force of logic or the attraction of a popular speaker. Paul is implicitly attacking the basis of the different parties within the community (v. 12).

TRUE WISDOM AND THE LANGUAGE OF LOVE. 2:6-3:4.

[6]Yet among the mature we do impart wisdom, although it is not a wisdom of this age or of the rulers of this age, who are doomed to pass away. [7]But we impart a secret and hidden wisdom of God, which God decreed before the ages for our glorification. [8]None of the rulers of this age understood this; for if they had, they would not have crucified the Lord of glory. [9]But, as it is written,

"What no eye has seen, nor ear
heard,
nor the heart of man conceived,
what God has prepared for those
who love him,"

[10]God has revealed to us through the Spirit. For the Spirit searches everything, even the depths of God. [11]For what person knows a man's thoughts except the spirit of the man which is in him? So also no one comprehends the thoughts of God except the Spirit of God. [12]Now we have received not the spirit of the world, but the Spirit which is from God, that we might understand the gifts bestowed on us by God. [13]And we impart this in words not taught by human wisdom but taught by the Spirit.

[14]The unspiritual man does not receive the gifts of the Spirit of God, for they are folly to him, and he is not able to understand them because they are spiritually discerned. [15]The spiritual man judges all things, but is himself to be judged by no one. [16]"For who has known the mind of the Lord so as to instruct him?" But we have the mind of Christ.

3 But I, brethren, could not address you as spiritual men, but as men of the flesh, as babes in Christ. [2]I fed you with milk, not solid food; for you were not ready for it; and even yet you are not ready, [3]for you are still of the flesh. For while there is jealousy and strife among you, are you not of the flesh, and behaving like ordinary men? [4]For when one says, "I belong to Paul," and another, "I belong to Apol'los," are you not merely men?

From the tone of this section it is clear that Paul is both replying to an objection and, at the same time, criticizing the attitude of one of the parties at Corinth. It would be more easy to determine exactly what he is trying to say if we had access to both sides of the conversation, but we can hear only Paul's. Attempts to reconstruct the Corinthian side of the dialogue have given rise to much controversy, but there is a growing consensus that it reflects the pattern of thought associated with Philo, the great Jewish philosopher of Alexandria, the city from which Apollos came (Acts 18:24-19:1).

Paul had told the Corinthians that in Christ they enjoyed a new mode of being (1:30) superior to that of those who were not believers. What precisely he meant by this will become clearer as we work through this letter. Here our concern is with the misunderstanding that arose at Corinth because some interpreted his words in a different mental framework. Instead of assimilating Paul's perspective they drew on the speculations of Hellenistic Judaism to fill out the meaning of his words. In consequence, they associated the idea of a superior plane of existence with the notions of 'wisdom' and 'perfection'. They thought of themselves as possessing a 'wisdom' which not only made them 'mature' or 'perfect', but which gave them the right to look down on others as 'babes'. They were 'spirit-men' (RSV 'spiritual') because they were dominated by the reasoning divine spirit, while these others were merely 'soul-men' (RSV 'unspiritual') animated by a principle of life directed to the satisfaction of the lower appetites. In substance, their 'wisdom' consisted in speculation on Christ as the 'Lord of Glory' and on the mysteries of the heavenly sphere in which he dwelt. They found it more convenient to ignore the historical dimension of his existence because the crucifixion offended their sensibilities.

These desired Paul to speak to them in terms appropriate to their intellectual and religious sophistication. He might content himself with simple proclamation to those capable of receiving nothing higher, but they expected much more. A latent note of challenge can be detected. If Paul did not offer them 'wisdom', might it not be that he was incapable of the soaring religious speculation that they took for granted? Might not the absence of such a gift indicate that he was not fitted to lead the community?

Paul was rather thin-skinned and rose at once to the bait. In the first part of his response (2:6-16) he takes on his opponents at their own game and shows that he can manipulate concepts as well as they. This little exercise in self-gratification is also designed to prick the bubble of their complacency because he completely changes the meaning of the terms they used. Since this should have left his adversaries in some confusion, the second part of his response (3:1-4) clearly articulates the basis of his objection to their attitude. In order to understand what he is getting at it is best to begin with the second part and then consider the first.

Paul's point in 3:1-4 is very simple. True christian perfection or maturity manifests itself, not in intellectual speculation, but in behaviour modeled on that of Christ (4:16-17; 11:1). When judged by this criterion the Corinthians appeared as only 'children' capable of assimilating nothing stronger than milk. Why? Because they accepted 'jealousy and strife' (3:3) and party factions (3:4) as part of the normal behaviour of a Christian. In Paul's eyes this showed that they were 'behaving like ordinary men' or, more literally, that they were 'walking according to man' (3:3). In the Apostle's vocabulary 'according to man' means 'according to the common estimation' (9:8; 15:32; Gal 3:14). In the world from which the Corinthians came jealousy, strife, and party factions were part and parcel of everyday existence, and to those who accepted the common estimation of what was possible to humanity it seemed entirely natural that they should be found within the community of believers. For Paul this was clear evidence of their immaturity. In Christ they had been given *the* standard by which authentic human behaviour was to be judged (2 Cor 5:15-18), but they had not used it. Hence, if wisdom was for the mature, Paul would talk wisdom elsewhere!

By comparison 2:6-16 is very complex. The reason is that Paul is there amusing himself by taking the terminology of his adversaries and using it in a sense which has the effect of reversing their position. He agrees that the Corinthians are 'spiritual' and have 'wisdom', but their spirit is 'the spirit of the world' (2:12), i.e. the value-system of their pagan environment, and their wisdom is 'the wisdom of this age' (2:6), i.e. based on conventional standards of judgment which cannot cope with the crucifixion. Hence, they are the ones who are 'unspiritual' and incapable of receiving 'the gifts of the spirit' (2:14). They are placed in the category of those whom they despised, and have no right to judge Paul (2:15).

True wisdom, on the contrary, must come from God because its content is the divine plan to save humanity through the crucifixion of Christ (2:7-8). This plan cannot be discovered by observation, nor can it be deduced from any principles available to human reason (2:9). It must be revealed by God (2:10). At this point Paul highlights the role of the 'spirit' in a way which has few if any parallels in the rest of his writings. He has to bring in the notion of 'spirit' because his opponents put such emphasis on it, but he transforms the meaning in order to serve his own purpose. His argument is based on human experience. We all experience the separateness of the other. In each person there are areas into which we cannot hope to penetrate either by observation or reason. Only the person's own self-consciousness ('spirit') is aware in such areas. Hence, in order to know what is going on in them we must be told. Similarly, Paul argues, only the divine self-consciousness ('spirit *of* God') can penetrate the depths of the divine mind, and this spirit must inform us if we are to know anything of God's thoughts (2:10-11). But it is also necessary that we be made capable of receiving this insight into the things of God by the gift of 'the spirit *which is from* God' (2:12 - compare the formulation with that of 2:11).

Revelation, however, is not direct. It is mediated by human agents chosen by God, of whom Paul is one (1:1, 17). Here Paul introduces a not very subtle polemic note. He preaches what God has revealed (2:6, 13). If some at Corinth refuse his preaching, the conclusion can only be that they have not received 'the spirit which is from God' (2:14). The language he uses is not that of the popular philosophy to which they are accustomed. He employs 'words taught by the spirit' (2:13). The closest parallel to this extraordinary expression occurs in 1 Thess 4:9, "But concerning brotherly love you have no need to have anyone write to you, for *you yourselves have been taught by God to love one another.*" Just as one type of knowledge, i.e. that which is rooted in a false value-system, is given with inauthentic existence ('the world'), so another type of knowledge is given with authentic existence ('the spirit'). Fallen humanity instinctively adopts the thought and language structures of its environment. Humanity's new being in Christ (1:30) is due to God's initiative and, in consequence, the instinctive knowledge given with it, and the language in which this knowledge is expressed, must be attributed to him. 'Words taught by the spirit' can be verbal but, in the light of 3:1-4, it seems clear that for Paul they were primarily existential. 'Those who love God', i.e. believers (2:9; 8:3; Rom 8:28), must express themselves in deeds rather than words (Mt 21:28-31). The behaviour of the Corinthians showed that they did not speak the language appropriate to their new being. Neither did they have 'the mind of Christ' (2:16) because it was concerned, not with speculation, but with obedience and service (Phil 2:5-7).

GOD'S CO-WORKERS.
3:5-9.

> ⁵What then is Apol'los? What is Paul? Servants
> through whom you believed, as the Lord assigned to each.
> ⁶I planted, Apol'los watered, but God gave the growth.
> ⁷So neither he who plants nor he who waters is anything,
> but only God who gives the growth. ⁸He who plants and
> he who waters are equal, and each shall receive his wages
> according to his labor. ⁹For we are fellow workers for
> God: you are God's field, God's building.

Up to this point in the letter Paul has been attempting to
deal with the divisions at Corinth by emphasizing the true
nature of the gospel (1:18-25) and the conditions for its
genuine reception (2:6-3:4). He now turns to another aspect.
Since the factions formed around different preachers (1:12;
3:4) he has to establish the authentic place and function of
such preachers. His development of this theme continues to
the end of ch. 4.

The absurdity of the Corinthian attitude is underlined by
the rhetorical questions which open the first sub-section (v.
5). The preachers are not 'masters' in their own right, but
'servants' of a higher authority on whom the Corinthians
should focus their attention. The preachers are not initiators
but instruments. Their function is to mediate faith which is
God's gift. In this sense Paul and Apollos are 'one' (v. 8 - not
'equal' as in RSV); their missions are directed to the same
goal. With regard to the specific community of Corinth,
however, there was a difference (v. 6). Paul sowed the first
seed (Acts 18:1; Rom 15:20) which Apollos nourished (Acts
18:17). Nonetheless the two roles were complementary and it
was ridiculous of the Corinthians to attempt to set them in
opposition to each other. Their veneration of individual
preachers had no basis in reality.

Paul's assertion that "neither he who plants nor he who
waters is anything" (v. 7) at first sight appears to contradict

his stress on the essential contribution of the preachers "through whom you believed" (v. 5). Absolutely speaking God has no need of human cooperation. Wild seeds are covered by wind-blown earth and flourish under the winter rains. Equally, God could have chosen to generate faith directly. In point of fact, however, he decided otherwise. He appointed intermediaries (v. 5), but not because they were in themselves capable of changing the human situation. They had to be empowered to achieve this effect (1 Thess 2:4; 1 Cor 15:10; 2 Cor 3:6; Gal 2:7-9). Everything, therefore, comes back to God (v. 6-7). Within the framework of the divine decision preachers are essential to the plan of salvation (Rom 10:14-17). They are truly 'God's co-workers' (v. 9 — not 'fellow-workmen for God' as in RSV; cf. 1 Thess 3:2) whose reward will be calculated, not on the basis of effort (as the 'labor', v. 8, of the RSV might imply), but on the basis of what is actually accomplished. Having dignified humanity by involving it in the execution of his plan of salvation, God will not be untrue to himself by by-passing the instruments he has chosen. If they fail, the divine power is rendered ineffective. Paul develops this theme in the next section.

GOD'S BUILDING.
3:10-23.

> [10]According to the commission of God given to me, like a skilled master builder I laid a foundation, and another man is building upon it. Let each man take care how he builds upon it. [11]For no other foundation can any one lay than that which is laid, which is Jesus Christ. [12]Now if any one builds on the foundation with gold, silver, precious stones, wood, hay, stubble—[13]each man's work will become manifest; for the Day will disclose, because it will be revealed with fire, and the fire will test what sort of work each one has done. [14]If the work which any man has built on the foundation survives, he will receive a reward.

¹⁵If any man's work is burned up, he will suffer loss, though he himself will be saved, but only as through fire.

¹⁶Do you not know that you are God's temple and that God's Spirit dwells in you? ¹⁷If any one destroys God's temple, God will destroy him. For God's temple is holy, and that temple you are.

¹⁸Let no one deceive himself. If any one among you thinks that he is wise in this age, let him become a fool that he may become wise. ¹⁹For the wisdom of this world is folly with God. For it is written, "He catches the wise in their craftiness," ²⁰and again, "The Lord knows that the thoughts of the wise are futile." ²¹So let no one boast of men. For all things are yours, ²²whether Paul or Apol'los or Cephas or the world or life or death or the present or the future, all are yours; ²³and you are Christ's; and Christ is God's.

The image underlying this section is that of a building. The shift from the planting image of vv. 5-9 is prepared for in the last part of v. 9, the association of the two images being common in Judaism (Jer 1:10; 12:14-16; 24:6; Ezr 17:1-8).

From the outset Paul makes it clear that he expects others to make contributions to the building whose foundation he laid (v. 10). The Christian community is an organic unity (12:12-31) in which everyone both gives and receives. On one level Paul is concerned to underline the positive relationship of his work and that of Apollos (3:6), but on another level he is preoccupied by the quality of the contributions made by the Corinthians (v. 10b). They prided themselves on their possession of 'wisdom' (v. 18), and obviously felt that as long as they were satisfied with their contributions all was perfect. Paul had already encountered their understanding of 'wisdom' (see on 2:6-3:4) and so was acutely conscious of the possibility of self-deception (v. 18a). The Corinthians' lack of true Christian wisdom betrayed itself in the way they exalted individual apostles (v. 21-22). They boasted of their commitment to particular leaders (3:4), and this permits Paul to turn the tables on them very neatly. The Corinthians, to a very great extent, drew their 'wisdom' from the environment in which they lived (v. 19), and one of the catch phrases of their world was the Stoic principle "All things belong to the wise man". If you really believed this, Paul implies, you would not say 'I belong to Paul or Apollos or Cephas', but rather 'Paul or Apollos or Cephas belong to me!' (v. 22). Having thus pricked the bubble of their complacency, Paul immediately becomes serious again and attempts to steer the thinking of the Corinthians in the right direction. The Corinthians had accepted Christ as 'the wisdom of God' (1:24), but gave this a meaning which did not coincide with that intended by Paul. However, the formula itself could serve Paul, because the Stoic principle accepted by the Corinthians permits him to say "you are Christ's" (v. 23). It is only because they are in Christ that the Corinthians have access to authentic knowledge (8:1-3) which continually tests itself by reference to Christ. He is the foundation with which all else must be homogeneous.

Paul's assertion of the foundation role of Christ appears in v. 11 which breaks the logical connection between v. 10b and v. 12a. This parenthesis was probably inspired by the claim of the Peter-party (1:12; 3:22) that Cephas was the 'rock' on which the community was founded (Mt 16:18) and that, in consequence, certain Jewish practices, notably in matters of food, must be observed in all churches. Paul did not deny the position of Peter (Gal 1:18) but he was not prepared to permit any confusion between the essential message of the gospel and the cultural accretions that had been part of its preparation (Gal 2:1-21). Only in and through their relation to Christ are believers saved, and Peter was the foundation only as the primary bearer of the witness on which the church rests.

To construct on the wrong foundation is only one way in which a builder can err, he can also go wrong by using inferior materials. Exactly what Paul has in mind in v. 12-15 is difficult to determine because of the fluidity of the images he uses. Nonetheless, the general thrust of his thought is clear. In the present there may be difficulties in discerning what is shoddy workmanship, but this will not be the case when 'the Day' arrives. Paul is here using the OT concept of the judgment Day of Yahweh (Is 2:12; Jer 46:10; Amos 5:18) to denote the Second Coming of Christ (5:5; 1 Thess 5:2; 2 Thess 2:2) which he believed to be very close. Fire is often associated with the Day of Yahweh (Joel 2:3; 3:3; Mal 4:1; Dn 7:9) and so with the Day of the Lord (2 Thess 1:7). This fire is not punishment; it will test the quality of the work of all (v. 13). That which survives is good, and that which is consumed is unworthy. It is noteworthy that Paul does not speak of condemnation. Even those whose work is consumed will be saved (v. 15). Shoddy workmanship, therefore cannot be equivalent to sinful attitudes, and so would appear to be a positive contribution that is less than the gifts accorded to each individual (12:4-11). Those who hoard their talents will barely escape with their skins (as a builder who dashes through the flames engulfing his shoddy edifice), but those who give to the limit of their gifts will be rewarded.

Worse than those who build with defective materials are those who would attempt to destroy the community (v. 17) by introducing elements incompatible with its basic character, viz. anything that smacks of egocentricity (see on 8:11-12). The rhetorical question introducing v. 16 implies a rebuke. The Corinthians should have had some insight into the nature of the christian community which, for Paul, was the basic reality, and in particular they should have seen the parallel between the community and the Temple in Jerusalem. This is the first time that Paul introduces the concept of the community as a spiritual temple. This theme appears elsewhere only in the Dead Sea Scrolls (*Rule of the Community* 8:4-10; 9:3-6), but it does not seem likely that Paul borrowed it from the Essenes. In opposition to the

Essenes Paul always associates the spiritual temple with the presence of the Spirit (v. 16; 6:19; 2 Cor 6:16). It is because "the Spirit of God dwells among you" that the community is analogous to the Temple in which God dwelt (Ps 74:2; Ez 9:3; 43:5-9; Hab 2:20). The temple was holy because it was 'set apart' for God's exclusive service. The community of believers is holy in the same way (see on 1:1-3), but this is intended only as a beginning. The opportunity of growth in freedom must be used to develop a pattern of behaviour which will make believers stand out as lights in the world (Phil 2:14-16). The holiness which is the fruit of love in action gives meaning to the title 'saints' given to believers (1 Cor 1:2; 2 Cor 1:1; etc.).

THE RIGHT ATTITUDE TOWARDS PASTORS. 4:1-5.

4 This is how one should regard us, as servants of Christ and stewards of the mysteries of God. [2]Moreover it is required of stewards that they be found trustworthy. [3]But with me it is a very small thing that I should be judged by you or by any human court. I do not even judge myself. [4]I am not aware of anything against myself, but I am not thereby acquitted. It is the Lord who judges me. [5]Therefore do not pronounce judgment before the time, before the Lord comes, who will bring to light the things now hidden in darkness and will disclose the purposes of the heart. Then every man will receive his commendation from God.

Paul takes up again the theme of 3:5-9 but from a different perspective. There he was content to state the true nature of the apostolate. Here he explicitly states the conclusion that the Corinthians should draw from what he said. The formulation of v. 1 in the RSV could give the impression that a new topic is being introduced, but the meaning is 'Thus we are to be regarded as....'

The preachers are defined as 'servants of Christ and stewards of the mysteries of God' (v. 1). 'Servant' here (*hypêrêtes*) is not the same word as in 3:5 (*diakonos*). There is a certain overlap in the meanings insofar as both designate a person in a subordinate position, but *hypêrêtes* had acquired a technical connotation in the language of the courts and the public service, namely, that of 'official witness' (Lk 1:1-4). The choice of this term furnishes us with a perfect example of Paul's astuteness because it highlights not only his subordinate role, but also his official position. A responsibility has been entrusted to him. Hence, he cannot pretend that he is independent or permit himself to be taken as an autonomous agent. Equally, he cannot let it be assumed that he is on the same level as the rest of the community, because he has the duty of ensuring the reliability of the view of Christ accepted by the believers. This aspect appears more explicitly in the term 'steward' because the stewards of the hellenistic kings occupied positions of great power in the administration of wide territories and the term was used to translate a Hebrew expression virtually equivalent to 'prime minister'. Paul is a subordinate but one to whom the execution of the plan of salvation ('the mysteries of God') has been entrusted.

Obviously, the key quality to be desired in such an administrator is absolute fidelity to the intention of him who commissioned him (v. 2). He is of no value unless he can be trusted to do precisely what is demanded of him. Hence, the only one competent to pass judgment on the behaviour of a 'steward' is the one who employs him. This is why Paul attaches no importance to any judgment that is not expressed by God (v. 3). The opinions of the Corinthians are without value; the judgments of any court are of no account. Even Paul's estimate of himself is irrelevant.

The way in which Paul expresses this last idea is highly significant. 'I am not aware of anything against myself' (v. 4) uses a Greek verb which is the cognate of the noun that we translate as 'conscience'. So we could translate the phrase by 'My conscience has nothing with which to reproach me'.

This is the first instance of the technical language of 'conscience' in the Pauline letters, although the underlying idea appears in 1 Thess 2:1-6, and it would appear that Paul assimilated it from the Corinthians. As we shall see in dealing with ch. 8, Paul could not accept the understanding of 'conscience' that the Corinthians maintained, but he had the insight to recognize that the concept could profitably be integrated into his theology. It would be a mistake, however, to imagine that Paul's concept is identical with the understanding of conscience prevalent in the church. He used 'conscience' only in the sense of 'pangs of conscience', i.e. the painful awareness of past transgressions, and there is no evidence that he envisaged 'conscience' either as the voice of God or as the agent of divine judgment. In fact, he here explicitly denies that the fact that his conscience gives him no pain means that God approves of his behaviour. The Lord will institute his investigation in his own way and in his own time.

'The time' (v. 5) is the moment when the Lord will come in judgment on humanity (11:26; Rom 2:16; 1 Thess 4:16; 2 Thess 2:8). "In view of this *last* judgment, all human verdicts must be *pre*-judice" (Barrett). Hence, the Corinthians should suspend judgment, and refrain from reaching any verdict. The reason for this can be inferred from the second part of v. 5; only the Lord knows the true intention of the heart which is the critical moral factor. If we simply take what Paul says here the meaning is limpid. A problem arises, however, when we confront this section with 5:1-8 where Paul is furious because the Corinthians did not condemn the incestuous man. The two positions can be reconciled, but only by a form of mental gynmastics of doubtful legitimacy, and it is perhaps best to say that Paul is not entirely consistent. As anyone who bears a heavy burden of responsibility (2 Cor 11:28) he was naturally most sensitive to attacks on his authority.

APPLICATION TO THE CORINTHIANS.
4:6-13.

> [6]I have applied all this to myself and Apol'los for your benefit, brethren, that you may learn by us to live according to scripture, that none of you may be puffed up in favor of one against another. [7]For who sees anything different in you? What have you that you did not receive? If then you received it, why do you boast as if it were not a gift?
>
> [8]Already you are filled! Already you have become rich! Without us you have become kings! And would that you did reign, so that we might share the rule with you! [9]For I think that God has exhibited us apostles as last of all, like men sentenced to death; because we have become a spectacle to the world, to angels and to men. [10]We are fools for Christ's sake, but you are wise in Christ. We are weak, but you are strong. You are held in honor, but we in disrepute.
>
> [11]To the present hour we hunger and thirst, we are ill-clad and buffeted and homeless, [12]and we labor, working with our own hands. When reviled, we bless; when persecuted, we endure; [13]when slandered, we try to conciliate; we have become, and are now, as the refuse of the world, the offscouring of all things.

The RSV version of v. 6 makes perfect sense, but the phrase 'to live according to scripture' hides one of the most controverted problems in the interpretation of this letter. A literal translation of the Greek would be '. . . that you may learn (the meaning of) "Not above what is written", that none of you . . .'. Efforts to make this yield an acceptable meaning are so speculative that it seems best to assume that at a very early stage a copyist omitted a 'not'. Another scribe, shortly afterwards, inserted the 'not' once again, but in the wrong place, and noted that it did not appear in the exemplar he was copying. What Paul wrote, therefore, was '. . . that you may *not* learn by our example to be puffed up, each on behalf of one and against the other.' In other words, there was nothing in the respective functions of Paul and Apollos (3:5-7; 4:1) which would justify either veneration or rivalry.

Nor did the Corinthians possess any native qualities which might tempt a preacher to recruit a following. The three rhetorical questions in v. 7 are designed to deflate the puffed up Corinthians. The first two expect a negative answer, and the third is a cutting conclusion which removes the ground from beneath their feet. Individually they have no distinguishing qualities which would make their adherence to a party a matter of any significance. What they do have that is really worthwhile was mediated to them by the preachers (3:5). Hence, there is no reason for them to feel proud of themselves. Paul is implicitly attacking the idea that preachers minister to the *taste* of an audience.

From sarcasm Paul turns to bitter irony (v. 8-10). In opposition to the preachers who are conscious only of suffering and struggle (v. 9), the Corinthians (who belong to the same church!) give the impression that they believe themselves to be in full possession of the eschatological Kingdom of God, enjoying its banquets, savouring its riches, and sitting on its thrones (v. 8). Paul's reaction: 'Would that this were true!' It would certainly make life easier for himself and his colleagues. The truth, of course, is that they have received only an earnest of what is to come (2 Cor 1:22; 5:5) and so must live by faith (2 Cor 5:7) because the End is not yet (15:24). The Corinthians had lost touch with reality. 'We *feel* ourselves to be fools, but you *think* yourselves wise. We *feel* ourselves to be weak, but you *think* yourselves to be strong. You *imagine* that you are held in honor, but we *know* ourselves to be held in disrepute.' (v. 10). In matters of religion experiential knowledge must be invoked to control speculation. To this end Paul highlights his own experience in a passage of deep sincerity (v. 11-13) which he intends to serve as an example (4:16) to the Corinthians. The beginning and end describe the factual conditions under which he, and others like him, actually work (2 Cor 4:7-12; 6:4-10; 11:23-33), whereas the central phrases outline his reaction to these conditions in words which are evocative of parts of the Sermon on the Mount (Mt 5:5, 10-11, 38-48; Lk 6:27-38).

AFTER SEVERITY SWEETNESS.
4:14-21.

> [14]I do not write this to make you ashamed, but to admonish you as my beloved children. [15]For though you have countless guides in Christ, you do not have many fathers. For I became your father in Christ Jesus through the gospel. [16]I urge you, then, be imitators of me. [17]Therefore I sent to you Timothy, my beloved and faithful child in the Lord, to remind you of my ways in Christ, as I teach them everywhere in every church. [18]Some are arrogant, as though I were not coming to you. [19]But I will come to you soon, if the Lord wills, and I will find out not the talk of these arrogant people but their power. [20]For the kingdom of God does not consist in talk but in power. [21]What do you wish? Shall I come to you with a rod, or with love in a spirit of gentleness?

Paul's severity in the last section was rooted in his concern for the Corinthians. Parents who have lost a child for several hours will know the feeling. But he recognizes the danger that he might have gone too far and adopts a conciliatory attitude. The change of tone is abrupt but extremely effective psychologically.

His purpose in writing is not to punish the Corinthians by reducing them to a state of abject shame. The harsh words are intended to be remedial because Paul cannot abrogate his responsibility. The nature of this responsibility, he feels, is not clear to the Corinthians. He is not to be put on the level of a 'schoolmaster' (RSV: 'guide'), i.e. one who merely teaches them things. This is indeed an aspect of the christian life, and there are many who can fulfil this role. He, on the contrary, brought them into being. 'I begot you through the gospel' (v. 15). He functioned as God's agent in the process which brought them from 'death' to 'life' (Col 2:13), i.e. from an inward-looking, self-centered nothingness (13:2) to a mode of being modeled on that of Christ who died 'that those who live might live no longer for themselves' (2 Cor 5:15). However, such an existential attitude is achieved only through personal decision. In accepting Christ the Corinthians had taken the first step but they still had a long way to go in terms of being really conformed to Christ. The purpose of Paul's paternal admonition is to dispose them to make practical decisions compatible with their theoretical commitment to Christ. Since the decision has to be personal (2 Cor 9:7) he can neither make it for them, nor impose it on them.

He cannot even offer very specific advice because of the complex variety of each one's daily life. The best he can do is to exhort them to try to remember how he behaved when he was with them, and then to do the same sort of thing themselves (v. 16). This theme of imitation appears in every letter whose recipients knew Paul personally (11:1; 1 Thess 1:6; 2:14; 2 Thess 3:7-9; Gal 4:2; Phil 3:17; 4:9) and betrays his conviction that those who dare to preach the present love of God in Christ must reveal Christ in their own personality (2 Cor 4:10). If the purpose of grace is to transform, then the credibility of those who proclaim the reality of grace demands that they have been transformed (2 Cor 3:18).

What Paul had heard of the behaviour of the Corinthians revealed that they had forgotten how Paul had behaved among them. Hence, he says that he has already sent Timothy (16:10; note the absence of his name in 1:1; compare 2 Cor 1:1) to remind them of his 'Christian way of life' (v. 17). Timothy was not only a trusted member of Paul's staff who had taken part in the evangelization of Corinth (2 Cor 1:19) but also, if we are to judge from the way Paul speaks of him, his closest friend (Phil 2:19-22). He frequently served as Paul's trouble-shooter in situations which required a combination of firmness and tact.

Perhaps Timothy's tact was more developed than Paul's which begins to evaporate at this point. The thought of what Timothy would be going into brought the situation of the community very clearly to mind, and his tone immediately becomes heated again (v. 18-21). He says in effect: Anyone would think that I was never again going to be among you; I shall come, and perhaps sooner than you think - then watch out when my power encounters your empty words! Paul may have intended to go at once, but God disposed otherwise, as 16:5-9 reveals. Once again he reminds the Corinthians that the reality of the Kingdom of God consists in evidence of transformation modeled on Christ (Rom 8:29), and not in empty speculation about doctrine.

Part II.

THE IMPORTANCE OF THE BODY.

5-6.

The Importance of the Body.
5-6.

HAVING DONE HIS BEST to deal with the divisions in the community, Paul now turns to more specific problems. As we shall see in the next section, some of these problems were brought to Paul's attention by the Corinthians themselves. Other facets of their life did not appear to them to give any cause for concern but when these came to Paul's attention, perhaps in the incidental conversation of Chloe's people (1:11) or other visitors (16:17), he felt obliged to take action.

Three such problems are dealt with in chs. 5 and 6:

1. A Case of Incest (5:1-13).
2. Lawsuits among Christians (6:1-11).
3. Casual Fornication with a Prostitute (6:12-20).

This arrangement reveals one of Paul's thought-patterns which also occurs elsewhere in the epistle. He starts with one topic, then shifts to another, and finally returns to the first but with a slight difference. This may be schematised as A-B-A'. Here we have sex - lawsuits - sex. This formal pattern, however, should not blind us to the underlying unity of these three sections. Each provides a concrete illustration of the Corinthian belief that no physical action has any moral significance (6:18b). Hence, in each Paul is concerned to convince them that body is the sphere in which commitment to Christ becomes real. There is no such thing as a purely spiritual christianity. The spirit must be enfleshed if believers are to imitate Christ.

A CASE OF INCEST.
5:1-8.

> **5** It is actually reported that there is immorality among you, and of a kind that is not found even among pagans; for a man is living with his father's wife. [2]And you are arrogant! Ought you not rather to mourn? Let him who has done this be removed from among you.
>
> [3]For though absent in body I am present in spirit, and as if present, I have already pronounced judgment [4]in the name of the Lord Jesus on the man who has done such a thing. When you are assembled, and my spirit is present, with the power of our Lord Jesus, [5]you are to deliver this man to Satan for the destruction of the flesh, that his spirit may be saved in the day of the Lord Jesus.
>
> [6]Your boasting is not good. Do you not know that a little leaven leavens the whole lump? [7]Cleanse out the old leaven that you may be a new lump, as you really are unleavened. For Christ, our paschal lamb, has been sacrificed. [8]Let us, therefore, celebrate the festival, not with the old leaven, the leaven of malice and evil, but with the unleavened bread of sincerity and truth.

Paul had told the Corinthians that in Christ they had been freed from the power of Sin which was identified with the pressures and standards of 'the world'. In order to maintain the feeling of being free the Corinthians deliberately set aside one of the most sacrosanct moral prohibitions of both Jews and pagans, namely, marriage with one's step-mother (v. 1). In their minds this rejection of societal norms was justified by their commitment to Christ who gave them access to a higher 'wisdom'. Consequently, they had only praise for the man who entered into an incestuous relationship 'in the name of the Lord Jesus' (v. 4: RSV translation inaccurate). They took pride in this evidence of their maturity and freedom (v. 2a, 6a).

As far as Paul is concerned they should have been deeply saddened. 'Should you not rather have gone into mourning (and shown the sincerity of your sorrow by taking the necessary steps) in order that he who has done this should be removed from among you.' (v. 2b). Paul does not say why the relationship was wrong, but we can infer at least part of his reason from his statement 'Be blameless both with regard to Jews and Greeks' (10:32). He envisaged the christian community as furnishing the existential affirmation (1 Thess 1:6-8; Phil 2:14-16) which demonstrated the reality of the message he preached. This function would be negated by behavior which offended the legitimate sensibilities of those whom the church had a mission to convert.

The implications of the Corinthian attitude were so clear that Paul's mood is one of impatience. He says in effect: 'Look, the consequences are so obvious, that even from a distance I have come to a decision! Why do you delay?' (v. 3). The slowness of the Corinthians was only one troublesome factor. The other was that Paul could not intervene directly and expel the sinner on his own authority. The basic assumption underlying this whole chapter is that the community alone had the right and the duty to make this decision (v. 2b; 2 Cor 2:6). Yet something had to be done, and so Paul avails himself of the only solution open to him. He stresses his spiritual presence in the community (v. 3-4), thus giving himself the right to speak without destroying the responsibility of the Corinthians. He hoped that his clear persuasive voice would swing them to his vision of reality; the truth of the community (v. 7) could be preserved only if the sinner were expelled.

If read carelessly Paul's decision appears brutal, but there is no doubt that he conceived such excommunication, not as a punishment, but as a remedy. The ultimate goal is the salvation of the individual, and it is important to perceive how Paul expected this to be achieved. Like his Jewish contemporaries Paul believed the world to be divided into two camps, the church controlled by God and the world dominated by forces hostile to God and personalized in the figure of Satan. 'Spirit' and 'flesh' (v. 5) correspond to this division. Neither of these terms is to be understood as designating part of the person. Each designates the whole person as viewed from different angles. 'Spirit' means the whole person as oriented towards God. 'Flesh' means the whole person as oriented away from God. In each case the orientation is revealed by behaviour.

Paul's hope was that the sinner would change his pattern of behaviour, and conceived excommunication as the stimulus that would produce this effect. He could afford to do so because he envisaged the christian community as a space inhabited by those who had 'put on love which binds everything together in perfect harmony' (Col 3:14). Anyone who had experienced the security, protection, and encouragement afforded by such love would, he believed, suffer severe pain when cast out into the cold egocentricity of the 'world'. The difference between the two modes of being would become inescapably clear, and the sharp sense of loss should force the sinner to recognize that the conduct which had merited the withdrawal of love was incompatible with genuine commitment to Christ. Once the 'flesh' had been 'destroyed' in this way, the 'spirit' was free to dominate. Once this point had been reached there is no obstacle to the return of the erring brother to full communion. Paul does not mention this in v. 5, but nothing in the verse excludes it. It is certainly illegitimate to interpret v. 5 as meaning that the sinner must be excluded until the last day, because 'salvation', for Paul, implies membership in the community.

The childish glee displayed by the Corinthians in flouting accepted standards (v. 6a) showed them to be immature (3:1-2), but it also revealed that they had failed to understand the true nature of the christian community and its relationship to authentic freedom. The community was intended to be a place where the behaviour of all was modeled on that of Christ (11:1). The consequent inspiration of good example, which stimulated authentic growth, was the barrier which prevented the bad example of the 'world' from influencing the believers. This is how they were freed from enslavement to Sin (Rom 6:17-18); they were no longer under pressure to conform to a false value-system.

Such being the case, we can understand Paul's insistence that every sin has a social dimension (v. 6b). The presence within the community of an attitude incompatible with Christ puts the freedom of all at risk because the protective barrier against the value-system of the 'world' (= 'Sin') has been weakened. In the case of incest the individual in question gave his personal pleasure more importance than the mission of the community. Such self-centeredness was a potent source of infection, and excision was the only solution. The behaviour of the other Corinthians, however, showed that they also had conserved attitudes related to the value-system of the 'world'. Paul was not so naive as to believe that such inherited attitudes were nullified by the act of conversion. They had to be consciously eradicated, and this was a task to which the Corinthians had to commit themselves in order to become what they were destined to be (v. 7). In order for their victory over Sin to become a reality 'malice and evil' had to be replaced by 'sincerity and truth' (v. 8).

In speaking of 'leaven' Paul draws on the ritual of the Jewish Passover. Leaven was used as a symbol of evil, and so in preparation for the feast every scrap of leaven or yeast had to be scrupulously removed from all houses. Once the feast of Unleavened Bread was over, new leaven was provided. For the Corinthians their turning to Christ was the dividing line between past ('old leaven') and present ('new leaven'). Hence, Paul underlines the urgency of the cleansing process by saying in effect, 'The paschal lamb has already been slain, and your house is not yet free of old leaven. You are late. Do something about it right now!' (v. 7b). This is the only occasion on which Paul speaks of the death of Christ as a 'sacrifice', and it should not be given undue importance by being taken out of context. In his intention it is designed to function merely as a temporal reference point in harmony with the image employed. Some scholars have thought that

Paul here uses Passover imagery because the feast was close at hand. This is not impossible, and it fits with the mention of Pentecost in 16:8, but such imagery would have formed part of the permanent mind-set of any Jew and would have been available at all times.

CLEARING UP A MISUNDERSTANDING. 5:9-13.

> [9] I wrote to you in my letter not to associate with immoral men; [10] not at all meaning the immoral of this world, or the greedy and robbers, or idolaters, since then you would need to go out of the world. [11] But rather I wrote to you not to associate with any one who bears the name of brother if he is guilty of immorality or greed, or is an idolater, reviler, drunkard, or robber—not even to eat with such a one. [12] For what have I to do with judging outsiders? Is it not those inside the church whom you are to judge? [13] God judges those outside. "Drive out the wicked person from among you."

As v. 13 clearly indicates this paragraph concerns the same case of incest, but Paul has become aware that something he had said in an earlier letter (now lost) might have contributed to the Corinthian error, and he now tries to clarify things by making an important distinction.

He had told the Corinthians not to associate with 'immoral men', and by this he meant any member of the community whose behaviour was incompatible with commitment to Christ. 'Immorality' is here used in an entirely generic sense. The Corinthians, however, either did not perceive the restriction or, as seems more likely, deliberately refused to see it in order to ignore the directive. In other words, they gave the directive such a rigorous meaning that it became incapable of fulfilment. Evil, they said, is everywhere, and the only way to avoid it is to leave the world completely. But this is impossible, they continued, and so we just have to live with it. Paul agrees, but only with regard to the 'world'. The church has to remain in contact with evil men because its mission is to convert them. The same is not true, however, of the christian community itself. It cannot fulfil its mission unless its pattern of behaviour is qualitatively better than that of the world. Hence, believers must avoid all social contact with those who are nominally Christians but whose conduct (v. 11) in no way differs from that of those under the dominion of Sin (v. 10). The specific vices listed by Paul either injure others or make one impervious to the needs of others and, in consequence, are incompatible with the love which is the essence of the christian life. Christians have been given a standard (the humanity of Christ) by which to judge themselves (v. 12). This criterion they must use, leaving the judgment of outsiders to God.

LAWSUITS AMONG CHRISTIANS. 6:1-11.

6 When one of you has a grievance against a brother, does he dare go to law before the unrighteous instead of the saints? [2]Do you not know that the saints will judge the world? And if the world is to be judged by you, are you incompetent to try trivial cases? [3]Do you not know that we are to judge angels? How much more, matters pertaining to this life! [4]If then you have such cases, why do you lay them before those who are least esteemed by the church? [5]I say this to your shame. Can it be that there is no man among you wise enough to decide between members of the brotherhood, [6]but brother goes to law against brother, and that before unbelievers?

[7]To have lawsuits at all with one another is defeat for you. Why not rather suffer wrong? Why not rather be defrauded? [8]But you yourselves wrong and defraud, and then even your own brethren.

[9]Do you not know that the unrighteous will not inherit the kingdom of God? Do not be deceived; neither the immoral, nor idolators, nor adulterers, nor homosexuals, [10]nor thieves, nor the greedy, nor drunkards, nor revilers,

nor robbers will inherit the kingdom of God. [11]And such were some of you. But you were washed, you were sanctified, you were justified in the name of the Lord Jesus Christ and in the Spirit of our God.

Paul has not yet finished all that he has to say regarding sexual morality among the Corinthians, and he returns to this topic in 6:12-20. The stress on judgment in 5:12-13 evoked another feature of the church at Corinth which caused difficulties for him. Disputes between Christians were being brought before pagan courts for judgment. Hence, he follows the association of ideas and deals with this topic here. The shift is not as abrupt as it appears at first sight because the principle which governed the Corinthian attitude towards sex, viz. behaviour has nothing to do with commitment, also underlies their position here. In response Paul makes two points: (a) there should be no disputes among believers (v. 7-11); (b) if such disputes should arise they should be dealt with within the community (v. 1-6).

The tendency of the Corinthians to separate conduct and commitment was related to their belief that they were definitively fixed in the state of salvation. For Paul, on the contrary, they were only in the process of 'being saved' (1:18), and the warning implied here in the juxtapositioning of v. 8 and 9 is made fully explicit in 10:1-22. The translation of the RSV should be modified to bring out this point: 'You do wrong...(v. 8)...wrongdoers will not inherit the kingdom of God (v. 9)'. As usual in Paul the list of vices (v. 9b-10) evokes the condition of humanity without Christ; all are but different aspects of the fundamental vice of selfishness. The Corinthians had once existed in this condition, but the baptismal rite of initiation had changed all that (v. 11). They had adopted another mode of being which was the antithesis of selfishness. In accepting Christ they had chosen the other-directed mode of being which he exemplified (Phil 2:6-7; 2 Cor 5:15). This they must live out in practice, for action is the only sphere in which commitment becomes real (Rom 6:19; 12:1-2; Gal 6:2).

Judged by this standard the Corinthians could only be considered failures (v. 7-8). The mere existence of disputes which necessitated the intervention of an impartial adjudicator proved that the selfish desire to acquire or retain had displaced the love which should characterise the relationship of believers. Life-giving love is what makes the believers members of one Body, and Paul underlines the destructive nature of such disputes in a very subtle way. He speaks of having 'lawsuits with your own selves' (v. 7, correct 'with one another' of RSV). So close was the relationship among believers that to bring suit against a fellow-member of the community was to bring suit against themselves. If some feel that they have been wronged or deprived, they should try to reform the one who has caused the injury. There is no place in the christian community for vindictive retaliation. Once again Paul echoes the Sermon on the Mount (Mt 5:39-42).

Despite his profound belief in the power of grace Paul had a very realistic view of what could be expected of people, and recognized that it took time for the effects of grace to make themselves manifest. The weakness of human nature, which had been dominated by Sin for so long, demanded that his new converts be given time to grow. It distressed him that it took so long, but there was no doubt in his mind about the principle. A community in which perfect harmony reigned was the ideal, but he did not think that such an ideal could be achieved instantaneously. He was even prepared to admit that individuals would need help to work through situations of friction. Such help, however, was to be sought within the community (v. 1-6).

Paul's insistence on this point is rooted in his conception of the mission of the church. A united community in which love dominates is the existential affirmation of the truth of the gospel. A community which contains within itself the divisions which characterise the 'world' has no power to transform its environment, because the contradiction between theory and practice is too evident (Rom 2:23-24). How much worse is it to deliberately bring such divisions to the attention of outsiders! (v. 1). It is not Paul's concern to organize a cover-up. He is not advising the pretence of a perfection that the community does not in fact enjoy. It is difficult to perceive true love in an absolutely tranquil situation; it becomes apparent only when there are tensions to be overcome. What Paul wanted the 'world' to see was a sincere effort on the part of the Corinthians to overcome the difficulties endemic to human life. To the extent that they were successful, outsiders could see the power of love in action.

In order to convince the Corinthians of the necessity of a change in their practice Paul employs two types of argument.

The first starts from a premise that the Corinthians would certainly accept, namely, 'The saints will judge the world' (v. 2). This was common Jewish doctrine (Wis 3:1, 8; Sir 4:11, 15; 1QpHab 5:3-4; Jubilees 24:29) which would appeal to the Corinthians' feeling of superiority. 'We are to judge angels' (v. 3) is only an extreme instance of the same principle, for angels were considered the highest order of beings in the universe (4:9). Given this premise Paul argues from the greater to the less. 'If the world is to be judged by you, are you unworthy of lesser tribunals?' (v. 2b). This formulation suggests that the Corinthians might have avoided getting involved in the affairs of their brethren on the grounds that they were unworthy to accept such a responsibility.

The second line of argument strips away this veneer of self-serving rectitude with a sarcastic scalpel. The Corinthians professed contempt for all those who did not have access to their exalted 'wisdom', i.e. those who did not belong to the community. Paul did not share this estimation; those who did not have the advantage of knowing Christ were to be pitied, not despised. Yet he accepts their view just in order to deflate the Corinthians. They accepted judgment from those whom they disdained! (v. 4). Having thus made his point Paul rubs it in with the ironic question, 'Among you, the wise, is there no one with sufficient wisdom to adjudicate the conflicting claims of his brethren?" (v. 5). The pretentiousness of the Corinthian self-image could hardly be displayed more cruelly.

CASUAL COPULATION
6:12-20.

> [12]"All things are lawful for me," but not all things are helpful. "All things are lawful for me," but I will not be enslaved by anything. [13]"Food is meant for the stomach and the stomach for food"—and God will destroy both one and the other. The body is not meant for immorality, but for the Lord, and the Lord for the body. [14]And God raised the Lord and will also raise us up by his power. [15]Do you not know that your bodies are members of Christ? Shall I therefore take the members of Christ and make them members of a prostitute? Never! [16]Do you not know that he who joins himself to a prostitute becomes one body with her? For, as it is written, "The two shall become one." [17]But he who is united to the Lord becomes one spirit with him. [18]Shun immorality. Every other sin which a man commits is outside the body; but the immoral man sins against his own body. [19]Do you not know that your body is a temple of the Holy Spirit within you, which you have from God? You are not your own; [20]you were bought with a price. So glorify God in your body.

The problem with which Paul deals here is that of casual copulation with a prostitute. We cannot be sure that this was a major problem at Corinth, because Strabo's story that the Temple of Aphrodite had more than a thousand sacred prostitutes has been shown to be pure fable. It seems natural to assume, however, that Corinth had its share of the problems that beset any port city. The section is of great importance, not for its obvious and inevitable conclusion, but because the problem forced Paul to give explicit attention to the christian attitude towards the physical body.

We have already had occasion to allude to the Corinthian attitude towards the body which underlay a number of their practical decisions. Here it comes out into the open because Paul actually quotes a number of statements made by the Corinthians. The section, therefore, is really a dialogue, and unless this is recognized it is very difficult to follow the argument. If we structure the text as a dialogue we get the following result:

Corinthians	*Paul*
(12) All things are lawful to me.	But not all things are expedient.
	But I will not be enslaved by anything.
(13) Foods are for the belly	The body is not for immorality but for the Lord,
and the belly for foods but God	and the Lord for the body, (14) but God
both one and the other will destroy.	both raised the Lord and will raise us by his power.
	(15) DO YOU NOT KNOW that your bodies are members of Christ?
	Shall I therefore take the members of Christ
	and make them members of a prostitute?
	Never!
	(16) DO YOU NOT KNOW that he who joins himself to a prostitute becomes one body with her?
	For it/he says, 'The two shall become one flesh.'

(17) But he who joins himself to the Lord is one spirit (with him).
Shun immorality.

(18b) Every sin which a man may commit is outside the body.

On the contrary, the immoral man sins against his own body.

(19) DO YOU NOT KNOW that your body is a temple of the holy spirit within you which you have from God?
You are not your own.

(20) You were bought with a price.
Glorify God through your body.

Let us look first at the Corinthian position. Their key argument is in v. 13 which can be restated in this way. The body has no permanent value because it is swept away by death. God concurs in this assessment because he permits the destruction of the body. Hence, anything done in and through the body has no moral value. Reformulated positively this means that 'All things are lawful' (v. 12). If no physical action has a moral character everything on the corporeal level is permissible. We can eat what we like and go to bed with whom we like.

This is not to say that the Corinthians denied the possibility of sin. Sin was possible but only on the level of motive and intention, and they refused to concede that these could be evaluated on the basis of the actions in which they were embodied. Hence, 'every sin which a man may commit is outside the body' (v. 18b) — not 'every *other* sin' RSV. For the Corinthians such sin was a purely theoretical possibility. They were so convinced of their own commitment that they did not consider sin to be a real possibility for themselves.

In his response Paul deals with the three Corinthian statements in turn, but he also introduces three statements prefaced by 'Do you not know' in which he draws out the implications (which the Corinthians should have seen for themselves) of teaching which he had already communicated to them.

Paul does not deny the statement 'All things are lawful to me' (v. 12). He may even have said something like that himself when explaining the believer's freedom from the multiple prohibitions of Jewish law. What he does is to attach two restrictions which bring it into line with his understanding of christian community. If taken literally the Corinthian principle implies the destruction of any community, and in particular a community founded on shared love, for it makes the self the standard. A thing is good because I want it. Conflict is inevitable because the desires of one will at some point encounter the needs or rights of the other. Hence, Paul has to point out that 'Not all things are expedient' (v. 12). Some courses of action tear the community apart, and thus destroy the very basis of the believer's freedom from the false value-system of the 'world'. If the community disintegrates, one is automatically returned to the state of enslavement to Sin (Rom 6:17-18). Naturally Paul rebels against this, 'I will not be enslaved by anything' (v. 12).

Having dealt with the consequences of the Corinthian principle, Paul then turns to its foundation, the moral irrelevance of the body. His response, which is structured to imitate the Corinthian formulation in v. 13, is a complete rejection of the Corinthian view. His basis is the fact that God raised Christ from the dead. This being the case, God will also raise those who are 'in Christ'. Now, if the body is to be the object of a divine action, if it is to benefit by a display of divine power, it cannot be unimportant in God's eyes, and so he must attach some significance to actions performed in and through the body. The body, therefore, is morally relevant, and Paul is forced to reject the Corinthian statement in v. 18b. 'On the contrary,' he says, 'the immoral man sins against his own body' (v. 18c), because he does not use it for the purpose intended by God. God brought humanity into existence to be the only creative creature (Gen 1-3). That creativity, whose goal was the effective opening-up of new possibilities of being for others, was to be expressed through the body which brought intention into the sphere of perception. It was wrong, therefore, to use the body for a non-creative purpose. In casual fornication with a prostitute the other person is not empowered to grow; the other is used for selfish gratification.

Confirmation of this interpretation is provided by the second 'Do you not know' statement (v. 16-17) where Paul quotes Gen 2:24, 'It/he says, "The two will become one flesh."' The speaker here could be God or Holy Scripture, but the point is hardly worth debating because for Jews there was virtually no difference. Scripture was the word of God. The divine purpose was that the act of intercourse should found a permanent union of two persons. They should become interdependent parts of a single entity. The act of intercourse, therefore, implies acceptance of responsibility for the other. Union with a prostitute, on the contrary, is intended to be transitory. Permanent commitment is positively excluded, and this is what makes it impossible for a Christian.

Having argued from the divine intention displayed in creation, Paul goes a step further in the two other 'Do you not know' statements: 'Your bodies are members of Christ' (v. 15) and 'Your [plural] body is a temple of the holy spirit within you [plural]' (v. 19). Here the christological dimension of human existence is highlighted because this was an aspect that the Corinthians were inclined to forget. They recognised Christ as the risen Lord of Glory (2:8) but ignored the implications of his historical existence. What God had achieved through Christ was brought about through his physical presence in the world. That physical dimension was essential to God's plan, so that authentic humanity could be seen as a real option, and not merely talked about as a beautiful ideal. By his resurrection Christ was removed from the sphere of the visible and tangible, but a visible and tangible representation of authentic humanity still remained imperative. In God's plan this demonstration was to be given by the christian community which Paul here calls 'Christ' (v. 15). The identity of the community with the historical Jesus is functional; the community continues the mission of Jesus. The 'bodies' of the Corinthians, therefore, are essential to their mission. Their physical presence in the world is intended to produce the same effect as that of Christ.

The commitment of the Corinthians to Christ is spiritual; they become one spirit with him (v. 17) because they are committed to what he desired. In order to enable them to achieve this goal they were given the holy spirit who empowers them to enflesh that unity of intention (v. 19). The statement 'Your [plural] body is a temple of the holy spirit within you [plural]' (v. 19) can be read in two ways. 'Body' can be understood as a distributive singular and thus as equivalent to 'bodies', or it can be understood as a true singular in which case the reference would be to the 'Body of Christ'. In the light of v. 15 the latter interpretation seems the more probable, particularly since 'You are not your own' (v. 19) is the complement of 'You are Christ's (3:23). Only together can Christians demonstrate the authentic humanity that Christ embodied because creative love binds those who give and those who receive into one. Those who display such love are as God intended them to be, and so 'glorify God in their body' (v. 20). It is only through membership in the Body that the believers become capable of honouring God. The ransom that Christ paid to make this possible (v. 20; Rom 3:24; Gal 3:13; 4:5) involved his body, and so their corporeity is the sphere in which the Corinthians must work out their salvation.

Part III.

RESPONSES TO CORINTHIAN
QUESTIONS.
7-14.

Responses to Corinthian Questions. 7-14.

THE FIRST VERSE of ch. 7 introduces a new series of problems, and the formulation - 'Now concerning the matters about which you wrote' - shows that these were issues concerning which at least some members of the community felt they needed Paul's advice. It is not clear in all cases whether they simply asked for his opinion or whether they outlined their solution and submitted it to him for approval.

The passage from one point to another is marked by the formula 'Now concerning X' which occurs at 7:25; 8:1, 4; 12:1, and in consequence the contents of this part of the letter can be divided into the following major sections:

1. Problems arising from social status (7:1-40) i.e. marriage, virginity, slavery.
2. Problems arising from the pagan environment (8:1-11:1) i.e. eating of idol-meats, participation in pagan banquets.
3. Problems arising in the liturgical assemblies (11:2-14:40) i.e. dress, Eucharist, spiritual gifts.

In dealing with these various topics Paul's discussion is often complex and sometimes tortuous, because he is concerned to keep all aspects of the problem in view. He has to show that he understands what the Corinthians are trying to do, while at the same time attempting to modify their approach so that it becomes more fully christian. In no case does he solve a problem by telling them what to do, because he did not believe that authority in the church should function that way (Philemon 8, 14). Authenticity is achieved only through personal decision and so he is by turns rational, emotional, persuasive, and passionate. The subtlety of his forthright personality is nowhere more evident.

1. Problems Arising from Social Status. 7:1-40.

Paul begins (7:1-16) and concludes (7:25-40) with a discussion of problems that are fundamentally sexual, but the center part of this section (7:18-24) is devoted to a consideration of the situation of circumcised/uncircumcised and of slave/freeman. Here, then, we have another instance of the A-B-A' pattern previously found in chs. 5-6. The association of the topics in this section may have been influenced by Paul's proclamation of the radical newness of the believer's new being in Christ, 'There is neither Jew nor Greek, there is neither slave nor free, there is no male and female, for you are all one in Christ Jesus' (Gal 3:28; Col 3:11).

SEXUAL RELATIONS IN MARRIAGE. 7:1-9.

7 Now concerning the matters about which you wrote. It is well for a man not to touch a woman. ²But because of the temptation to immorality, each man should have his own wife and each woman her own husband. ³The husband should give to his wife her conjugal rights, and likewise the wife to her husband. ⁴For the wife does not rule over her own body, but the husband does; likewise the husband does not rule over his own body, but the wife

does. [5]Do not refuse one another except perhaps by agreement for a season, that you may devote yourselves to prayer; but then come together again, lest Satan tempt you through lack of self-control. [6]I say this by way of concession, not of command. [7]I wish that all were as I myself am. But each has his own special gift from God, one of one kind and one of another.

[8]To the unmarried and the widows I say that it is well for them to remain single as I do. [9]But if they cannot exercise self-control, they should marry. For it is better to marry than to be aflame with passion.

In trying to understand this section it is extremely important to keep in mind that Paul is not talking about marriage as such. He is replying to a Corinthian position, and what he says is conditioned by what they have said. They proposed that 'It is good for a man not to have sexual intercourse with a woman' (v. 1b). There was here an element of idealism that struck a chord in Paul. He himself lived a life of sexual asceticism (v. 7-8), and he personally believed that someone like him could give undivided attention to the Lord (v. 32-35), and live a more ordered (v. 35), less anxious (v. 32), less troubled (v. 28), and happier life (v. 40).

There can be little doubt that Paul was convinced that his way of life was better than the married state. This made it inevitable that he should counsel others to do likewise (v. 8), but he did not fall into the trap of imagining that what was best for him was best for everyone else. He was keenly aware of the danger of transferring a theoretical ideal to a concrete situation, and of the cruelty inherent in trying to create instant perfection by fiat. This is what the Corinthians had failed to perceive, and Paul's major concern is to moderate their ascetic impulse by injecting a note of realism.

He takes it for granted that there is nothing morally wrong either with marriage or with sexual relations within marriage. This is nowhere explicitly stated, presumably because the Corinthians did not disagree. Their fault here was an exaggerated idealism which led them to try and impose practical acceptance of the ideal on all. In response Paul simply asks them to look at reality. He points out that they are not living in a perfect world but in an environment full of allurements to forbidden sex (v. 2a). He underlines too that many have such a strong sex drive that it can become a major distraction, if not a pitfall, when the legitimate satisfaction of marriage is denied (v. 9). To impose celibacy on such people would be to defeat the ideal, because they would not in fact be freed to devote themselves to the Lord. Boiling frustration is the only consequence that any sane person could expect. The practice of celibacy, therefore, should be proposed only to those who show signs of having been gifted by God for this way of life (v. 7b).

Those who are in fact married show by this fact alone that they have not been called by God to celibacy. Hence, they should have normal sexual relations (v. 3). In this context Paul speaks of 'conjugal rights', or more literally 'the debt'. If at first sight this should seem a cold legalistic approach to marriage, it helps to envisage the sort of situation that Paul had in mind. He was thinking of a marriage in which one partner had accepted the idea that permanent abstinence from sex was the ideal, but the other had not. Was one partner, then, to be forced into celibacy because the other had chosen it? Paul's answer is a resounding no. It is for this reason that he introduces the idea of 'debt' (v. 3) which he substantiates in v. 4. Marriage is a mutual gift; the body of each is given to the other. This gift is part fact and part promise, and it is this latter aspect which gives rise to the idea of 'debt'. Something is owed to the other. Obviously, then, such an obligation cannot be unilaterally renounced.

If there is to be abstinence from sex within marriage it must be by mutual agreement (v. 5). It cannot be legitimized by the appeal of one partner to a higher ideal. In this Paul is in reaction against the Jewish practice whereby a man could vow to avoid cohabitation for a while in order to devote himself to study or prayer without consulting his wife. Paul refuses the exclusiveness of the male decision, and insists on the equality of husband and wife in this regard, because the purpose of the agreement is that both may devote themselves to prayer (v. 5). It is not to be thought that prayer was the only objective that would justify a mutual agreement not to have sex. Paul was fighting against a doctrinaire attitude that could destroy a marriage. Hence, he insists that the partners have a specific goal (of which prayer is but one example) and a time limit. He is assuming that they do not have the gift of celibacy, and so he advises them to attempt only what is feasible. To reinforce this he underlines the very real possibility of temptation if individuals overestimate their strength.

The language that Paul uses here is very categorical. Phrases such as 'the husband/wife should give', 'do not refuse one another', and 'come together again' have the ring of imperatives, and Paul was aware that what he was saying might be taken as a matter of binding obligation by the Corinthians. This would make him as doctrinaire as they. Even worse, it would be a misunderstanding of how he believed authority should be exercised in a christian community (2 Cor 8:7-8; 9:7; Philem 8, 14). Hence, he explicitly states that nothing he has said should be taken as a 'command' (v. 6). It should, on the contrary, be understood as a 'concession'. This is a technical term familiar to Paul from his rabbinic training and denotes a position that owes more to an understanding of the real possibilities open to humanity in its concrete historical situation than to a theoretical ideal. Paul recognised the weakness of human nature. This might appear to be condescending but there was little choice for one who preferred realism to illusion. The Corinthians chose to forget that the imposition of a difficult ideal was more likely to produce frustrated despair than perfection. Paul did not, because his concern was that others might grow. But circumstances might change. Individuals might be stronger than he anticipated. This is why Paul leaves them free and underlines the factual nature of his assertions.

MARRIAGE AND DIVORCE.
7:10-16.

> [10]To the married I give charge, not I but the Lord, that the wife should not separate from her husband [11](but if she does, let her remain single or else be reconciled to her husband)—and that the husband should not divorce his wife.
>
> [12]To the rest I say, not the Lord, that if any brother has a wife who is an unbeliever, and she consents to live with him, he should not divorce her. [13]If any woman has a husband who is an unbeliever, and he consents to live with her, she should not divorce him. [14]For the unbelieving husband is consecrated through his wife, and the unbelieving wife is consecrated through her husband. Otherwise, your children would be unclean, but as it is they are holy. [15]But if the unbelieving partner desires to separate, let it be so; in such a case the brother or sister is not bound. For God has called us to peace. [16]Wife, how do you know whether you will save your husband? Husband, how do you know whether you will save your wife?

This section falls into two parts. In v. 10-11 Paul deals with a marriage in which both partners are Christians, and in v. 11-16 with marriages in which only one partner is a believer. The problem of divorce is common to both, but in the first case an actual situation had developed at Corinth, while in the second the Corinthians only suggest a proposed course of action to Paul.

To deal with the first case Paul brings forward a directive stemming from Jesus which prohibits divorce. This text is found in Mt 5:31-32; 19:9; Mk 10:11-12; Lk 16:18. In Mt and Lk all attention is concentrated on the man, which is what we would expect, because in Jewish law only the husband could initiate divorce proceedings. According to the Mishnah, 'A woman goes out whether she likes it or not, but the husband sends her out only if it so pleases him.' (Yebamoth 14:1). A woman could petition the court to put pressure on her husband to give her a divorce, but the court itself had no authority to break up the marriage. Among Greeks and Romans, however, the wife had the right of divorce, and Mk 10:11-12 shows how the directive of Jesus was expanded to cover this new situation. Paul's version does not agree verbally with any of the three Synoptics, but is closest to Mt and Lk insofar as it assumes that only the husband has the right of divorce. This is not clear in the RSV which mistranslates v. 10. The correct translation is 'the wife should not *be separated* from her husband', i.e. the wife should not accept a writ of divorce. This element does not appear in the directive of Jesus but it is the necessary passive complement to the active element in v. 11b.

The parenthetical statement (v. 11b) is Paul's application of the directive to a specific situation, and once again the RSV translation 'if she does' must be corrected to 'if she should be separated'. We have no hard information as to what was going on in this particular marriage, but the following reconstruction gives all the elements of the text their full value, and shows why Paul passed from the topic of v. 1-9 to this problem. The husband had been influenced by the ascetics who proclaimed, 'It is good for a man not to have sexual intercourse with a woman' (v. 1b), but instead of simply abstaining, he decided to break up the marriage completely by divorcing his wife. The wife, it is presumed, did not share his views. Naturally, then, she would think in terms of a second marriage, because the essential element in a writ of divorce was the right to marry again. Paul hoped that the husband would give serious attention to what he had just said in the previous paragraph (v. 1-9) and, if that did not convince him, that he would respect Jesus' prohibition of divorce. Paul did not have to worry about remarriage in the husband's case, because the motive for the divorce excluded it. But should the husband come to his senses, there could be an extraordinary mess if the wife had already committed herself to another man. Hence, Paul tells the wife (a) not to accept the writ of divorce, and (b), if it should be forced on her, not to consider herself free to remarry. As a Christian she should think only in terms of reconciliation with the one who had injured her. In this case, therefore, Paul applies the directive of Jesus strictly because he did not recognise the validity of the grounds for the divorce. He comes to a radically different decision in the second case to which he now turns.

In order to make sense of v. 12-16 we have to assume that some people in the church at Corinth were insisting that marriages in which only one partner was a Christian should be broken up. Why they should have adopted this attitude becomes clear if we recognise that Paul had insisted that the quality of life of the community was the basis of its freedom from enslavement to the false value-system of the 'world'. A sinner in the community was a threat to all (see on 5:6-7). An unbeliever was by definition a sinner, and so the question inevitably arose: could the community tolerate the presence by marriage of a sinner? Given the theoretical approach of the Corinthians a negative answer was inevitable.

Not having any sympathy with such a doctrinaire attitude Paul responds with a distinction. There are mixed marriages in which the unbeliever is content to live with the convert, and there are mixed marriages where the unbeliever refuses cohabitation. In each case a different decision must be made.

Where the unbeliever consents to live with the convert there should be no divorce (v. 12-13). Note that here Paul reflects a non-Jewish situation because the woman has the right of divorce. It is this factor which influenced the RSV translation of v. 10. The apparent inconsistency arises because Paul was faithful both to what Jesus actually said in a Jewish environment and to what actually went on in the wider world. Paul's reason for refusing divorce in this instance is the possibility of conversion, 'Think of it: as a wife/husband you may be the salvation of your husband/wife' (v. 16). The believer who exhibits the wholeness of authentic humanity is an existential call to salvation, as 1 Pt 3:1-2 shows so beautifully. Given the minimum good-will shown by the consent to live with the convert, Paul saw the unbelieving partner as drawn within the sphere of apostolic influence of the community through the contact provided by the believer, and refused to admit that he or she was a danger to the community. On the contrary, he says, 'the unbelieving husband/wife is sanctified through his wife/her husband' (v. 14a).

For Paul this is an unusual use of the concept of 'sanctity'. Elsewhere he applies it only to believers (e.g. 1:2; 6:11) and it is equivalent to being in the state of salvation. It is clear, however, that such static 'sanctity' must be realised in a pattern of behaviour appropriate to the new being of the believers (7:34; 2 Cor 1:12; Rom 6:19-22; 12:1-2; 1 Thess 3:12-13; 5:23). In the case under consideration the unbeliever was doing exactly what Paul hoped believers would do. By consenting to maintain the marriage the unbeliever was affirming the divine intention for marriage (Gen 2:24 quoted in 6:16), and was obeying Jesus' prohibition of divorce (v. 10-11). In terms of his behaviour-pattern, therefore, he was 'holy', and for this Paul gives the credit to the quality of the relationship developed by the convert partner.

Since Paul did not normally predicate 'sanctity' of behaviour which was not accompanied by the commitment of faith (2 Thess 2:13-14), he had to make sure that the Corinthians understood him. To this end he adduces the example of their children. He says in effect, 'If you don't accept what I have been saying, you have to say that your children are unclean. In fact, however, you rightly consider them to be holy' (v. 14b). For the illustration to achieve its goal the children have to be in a situation parallel to that of the unbeliever. This is verified if we assume them to be too young for the mature decision of faith. In a sense, therefore, they were 'unbelievers'. Yet the Corinthians did not think for a minute of expelling them. Why? Because their behaviour (influenced by their believing parents) revealed, not the 'uncleanness' typical of the 'world' (Rom 6:19; 1 Thess 4:7), but the 'holiness' of those in Christ. Just as the Corinthians hoped that their own children would grow into faith, so they should accord the same opportunity to the unbeliever. To insist on divorce in this instance would be to contradict the mission of the community.

The situation is quite different when the unbelieving partner refuses to live with the convert, and Paul expresses himself without ambiguity, 'If the unbelieving partner issues a writ of divorce, then let the divorce stand' (v. 15a). In such cases, Paul continues, the Christian is not to be the slave of a relationship that the unbeliever wants to abandon. Otherwise there would be continuous strife, a permanent distraction, whereas the purpose of God's call is peace (v. 15c). In this instance, therefore, Paul permits a true divorce with the consequent right of remarriage. His prohibition of remarriage in v. 11 is limited to the particular case he there has in mind, and must not be understood as a general principle.

Paul's decision here, then, is in flat contradiction to Jesus' prohibition of divorce (v. 10-11). It cannot be claimed that Jesus' prohibition concerned only christian marriages, and so is inapplicable in the case of mixed marriages. Jesus issued his directive to Jews (Mt 19:3, 9; Lk 16:14, 18) and based his argument on the intention of the Creator (Mt 19:4-6; Mk 10:6-9). His directive, therefore, is valid for all marriages. Yet Paul did not obey, thus showing that he did not understand the directive of Jesus as a binding precept. It was an important expression of the ideal, and Paul underlines its permanent value by using the present tense (v. 10a), but he refused to impose the ideal indiscriminately. The ideal embodied in Jesus' prohibition was designed to illuminate and inspire, not to be used as a stick to beat the weak and unfortunate.

CHANGES IN SOCIAL STATUS.
7:17-24.

> [17]Only, let every one lead the life which the Lord has assigned to him, and in which God has called him. This is my rule in all the churches. [18]Was any one at the time of

his call already circumcised? Let him not seek to remove the marks of circumcision. Was any one at the time of his call uncircumcised? Let him not seek circumcision. [19]For neither circumcision counts for anything nor uncircumcision, but keeping the commandments of God. [20]Every one should remain in the state in which he was called. [21]Were you a slave when called? Never mind. But if you can gain your freedom, avail yourself of the opportunity. [22]For he who was called in the Lord as a slave is a freedman of the Lord. Likewise he who was free when called is a slave of Christ. [23]You were bought with a price; do not become slaves of men. [24]So, brethren, in whatever state each was called, there let him remain with God.

If we were to look for a common denominator underlying the various Corinthian attitudes that came to light in 7:1-16 it would be the belief that their relationship with God could be improved by a change in social status. The married would be better if they were celibate. Those in mixed marriages would be better if they were single. Paul's response was (a) that no social change should be initiated for the sake of principle; (b) that a social change could be initiated to compensate for a human weakness; (c) a social change initiated by factors outside one's control could be accepted. This being the case, the transition to v. 17-24 appears very natural, because there he is concerned with parallel types of social change, and comes to the same conclusions.

The principle that a socio-legal change should not be initiated for the sake of principle is applied to those who have or do not have the mark of circumcision (v. 18). Instances are known of Jews, who had abandoned their faith, undergoing operations to restore the foreskin (1 Macc 1:15). The same principle is applied to those who were converted as slaves (v. 21), but here an exception had to be made because slaves were not in control of their own destiny. They could not decide to be free; it was something that happened to them. Hence, if their master decided to free them, they had to accept it; the change was due to factors outside their control.

Paul's argumentation here is much more theological than in 7:1-16 where his decisions were based on pragmatic considerations. The fact that God's call comes to individuals in all sorts of very different socio-legal situations shows such situations to be essentially irrelevant. God's call is not motivated by wealth or poverty, by intelligence or ignorance. It would be absurd, therefore, to imagine that a social change has the automatic effect of raising one in God's estimation. Christians, in consequence, should not waste any time worrying about their social position or planning a change.

Paul uses 'call' as a technical term for the process of salvation. It is always God who 'calls' and this act puts the divine plan of salvation into action (Rom 8:28-30). The 'call', then, is motivated by 'the immense love wherewith he loved us' (Eph 2:4-6), and the only adequate response to this summons is 'the obedience which is faith' (Rom 1:5). The concern of the believer should be to translate this obedience into a pattern of behaviour appropriate to their new being in Christ. Paul does not spell out precisely what this involves. He mentions only 'keeping the commandments of God' (v. 19b). In view of his own attitude towards the directive of Jesus prohibiting divorce, Paul cannot mean a servile submission to a code of law. The new law is Christ (9:21; Gal 6:2) or the Spirit (Rom 8:2), which can be crystallised in the commandments to love God and one's neighbour (Rom 13:9; Gal 5:14). It is to this that Christians should give all their energies, and there are multiple opportunities to love in every type of socio-legal situation. Only by availing themselves of such opportunities can they really improve their relationship with God.

This being the case, everyone could see the irrelevance of the presence or absence of a particle of skin (v. 19). These were symbols which had lost all meaning. The advent of Christ, who is 'the power of God and the wisdom of God' (1:24), brought about a completely new situation, in which much that was once relevant has lost all validity.

The 'slave-freeman' relationship demanded a little more explanation. Here Paul juggles with words (v. 22) and his purpose is to show the absurdity of thinking in terms of social labels. One whose social position is that of a slave is nonetheless 'a freedman of the Lord'. In Greek law a slave lacked the four freedoms: freedom to act as one's own legal person, freedom from seizure as property, freedom to choose one's employment, freedom to decide one's dwelling-place. A slave who became a freedman did not automatically acquire all these freedoms. Except in very rare cases a number of restrictions remained. Even while remaining a slave the believer had acquired certain freedoms. He had been freed from Sin (Rom 6:17) i.e. from the compulsion to conform to the false value-system of the 'world'. In consequence, he had also been freed from the Law (Rom 6:14), i.e. from an inherited attitude commanding blind obedience to precepts, and from 'death' (15:54-57), the egocentric mode of being which is the antithesis of 'life' in Christ (Col 2:13).

Equally, one who is legally a freeman is nonetheless 'a slave of Christ' (v. 22) because he is committed to 'the obedience which is faith' (Rom 1:5). He 'belongs to Christ' (3:23), no longer to himself (6:19). He is no longer an independent entity, but a member of the Body (6:15; 12:12-27).

The slave has been bought (v. 23) into a limited freedom, and the freeman has been bought into a limited servitude. Nothing could demonstrate more clearly how ridiculous it is to give the terms 'slave' and 'free' an absolute value.

In speaking as he does in v. 17-24 it is not clear if Paul is dealing with a real situation. This section can be adequately explained as pure illustration of the position he has taken in v. 1-16 and will take in the rest of the chapter. It is equally possible, however, (given the doctrinaire attitude of the Corinthians), that some in the community took a stand in principle, guided by Paul's own teaching, 'there is neither Jew nor Greek, there is neither slave nor free' (Gal 3:28). Paul intended this as a rejection of social status, not as a program of social action, but misinterpretation came easily to the Corinthians. If this were in fact the case, Paul would be concerned to dampen the enthusiasm of a social revolution which could not be completed before the Parousia (v. 29, 31) — one-third of the population of Corinth were slaves, and another third freedmen — and which could compromise the credibility of christian witness, because it would be a frontal attack on the economic stability of society. In view of what Christ had done for us Paul was quite capable of demanding similar sacrifices both of himself (2 Cor 11:24-28) and others.

CHANGES IN SEXUAL STATUS.
7:25-40.

²⁵Now concerning the unmarried, I have no command of the Lord, but I give my opinion as one who by the Lord's mercy is trustworthy. ²⁶I think that in view of the impending distress it is well for a person to remain as he is. ²⁷Are you bound to a wife? Do not seek to be free. Are you free from a wife? Do not seek marriage. ²⁸But if you marry, you do not sin, and if a girl marries she does not sin. Yet those who marry will have worldly troubles, and I would spare you that. ²⁹I mean, brethren, the appointed time has grown very short; from now on, let those who have wives live as though they had none, ³⁰and those who mourn as though they were not mourning, and those who rejoice as though they were not rejoicing, and those who buy as though they had no goods, ³¹and those who deal with the world as though they had no dealings with it. For the form of this world is passing away.

³²I want you to be free from anxieties. The unmarried man is anxious about the affairs of the Lord, how to please the Lord; ³³but the married man is anxious about worldly affairs, how to please his wife, ³⁴and his interests are divided. And the unmarried woman or girl is anxious about the affairs of the Lord, how to be holy in body and spirit; but the married woman is anxious about worldly

affairs, how to please her husband. [35]I say this for your own benefit, not to lay any restraint upon you, but to promote good order and to secure your undivided devotion to the Lord.

[36]If any one thinks that he is not behaving properly toward his betrothed, if his passions are strong, and it has to be, let him do as he wishes: let them marry—it is no sin. [37]But whoever is firmly established in his heart, being under no necessity but having his desire under control, and has determined this in his heart, to keep her as his betrothed, he will do well. [38]So that he who marries his betrothed does well; and he who refrains from marriage will do better.

[39]A wife is bound to her husband as long as he lives. If the husband dies, she is free to be married to whom she wishes, only in the Lord. [40]But in my judgment she is happier if she remains as she is. And I think that I have the Spirit of God.

This is probably the most difficult and controverted section of the letter. There are many different interpretations, and none of them is immune to objections. This obscurity is due to the fact that we have no very clear idea of what the Corinthian position was. We are not reduced to pure conjecture, but the evidence is so slight that it can legitimately be interpreted in different ways. However, despite the high degree of uncertainty, it is imperative to develop a hypothesis presenting the Corinthian position, because otherwise Paul's response will remain largely unintelligible.

It is certain from v. 25 that Paul here passes to a new question proposed by the Corinthians. The heading (v. 25) mentions 'virgins' (RSV 'unmarried') but the section in fact contains quite a few references to marriage. Most notable is Paul's insistence that marriage is not a sin (v. 28, 36). When dealing with 7:1-16 we did not catch the slightest hint that the Corinthians thought marriage to be wrong. Hence, we have to assume that their question here concerned individuals for whom marriage was thought to be sin because of a special commitment that they had undertaken. In other words, Paul was faced with a situation in which individuals had committed themselves to celibacy in marriage. This is quite different from the situation envisaged in 7:1-9 where individuals expected normal sexual expression within marriage. The ascetics at Corinth would have been operating on two fronts. On the one hand, they tried to persuade married couples to forego sexual relations, while on the other hand they tried to convince engaged couples to enter into a spiritual marriage. That they had some success with at least one married couple is suggested by 7:11, and it is possible that the present question arose because some who had chosen spiritual marriage found it to be beyond their strength.

A very definite light is thrown on v. 25-40 if we assume that Paul is speaking, not of normal marriage as such, but of spiritual marriages. But still a question remains. Did the letter from Corinth argue in favour of such marriages or against such marriages? It would be unrealistic to imagine that all members of the Corinthian community thought alike on all issues, and 8:1-13 in fact proves the contrary. Hence, it is not at all impossible that the question that Paul here tries to resolve came from a group opposed to those who wrote 7:1. In fact we do more justice to the complexity of Paul's answer if we assume this to be the case.

Our hypothesis, therefore, is that some members of the community at Corinth informed Paul of their opposition to spiritual marriages, and may have gone on to substantiate their point by presenting the difficulties of a particular case.

The framework of Paul's response is provided by his two statements, 'the appointed time has grown very short' (v. 29a) and 'the form (the social and commercial institutions) of this world is passing away' (v.31b). These show that Paul believed that the Second Return of Christ was imminent (1 Thess 4:13-18), and he assumes the Corinthians to be aware of it too. From it they should have made some obvious deductions. They evidently had not, and so Paul proceeds to do so with a laborious patience that but thinly disguises his frustration.

In the first place, they should not imagine that the realities that make up the fabric of their present lives are going to endure for very long. This is the central thrust of v. 29b-31a whose individual phrases should not be taken out of this context. Paul is not recommending that husbands should cease to love their wives (v. 29b), nor that they should put on a hypocritical show of sorrow or rejoicing, nor that they stop all commercial activity. His concern is to prepare them for the day when all these will change. He is asking for an attitude of detachment from the dear, familiar things which tend to absorb humanity. It is foolish to give too much importance to the impermanent.

In the second place, the Corinthians should have the wit not to involve themselves in the complexities of a change of sexual status at a moment when the imminent approach of the end will bring inevitable difficulties (v. 26). Paul, therefore, argues for the retention of the status quo of each individual. The married should stay married (v. 27a). The single should stay single (v. 27b, 39-40). Those in spiritual marriages should maintain their commitment (v. 37).

In this tolerance we find a clear echo of Paul's conviction that social status has no relevance (7:17-24), but it seems legitimate also to detect the assumption that a freely chosen state of life betrays the presence of a God-given charism (7:7). In this perspective, to decide to change one's chosen status might appear to be rebellion against God. As we might expect, however, Paul gives the greatest weight to the voice of experience. Change means trouble, and in particular the change from the single to the married state (v. 28b, 32-34).

At first sight this appears rather one-sided, but we have to recollect that Paul has reacted equally strongly against any tendency to move from the married to the single state (7:1-16). It must also be kept in mind that Paul is not speaking about marriage as such, but of marriage within the context of the Corinthian community where feelings were running very high. Those who married would certainly come under attack from the ascetics, and would have to waste a lot of energy in repulsing their futile advances ('worldly troubles' v. 28b; 'worldly affairs' v. 33-34). They would be distracted by matters that have absolutely no importance. Equally, the newly married would have to give time to pleasing their partner (v. 33-34). Paul's implicit condemnaton of this attitude is one of the more shocking statements in the letter and easily lends itself to misinterpretation. Since he made love the basis of the christian life (13:2), Paul cannot see involvement with another person as a distraction from the affairs of the Lord. The very next chapter highlights the supreme importance of such concern, and emphasises the barren self-deception of a commitment to God which does not embody such practical concern for the other. He is thinking here of the total absorption of the newly married, and what he is trying to get across (admittedly not very well) is the egocentric character of this attitude. A husband or wife has the first, but not the exclusive, claim on one's love. One must remain open to others. In serving others with whom one is not emotionally involved one can be (and very often is) conscious of the relationship to God. It would be naive to expect to find any such reference in the sexual excitement of a newly married couple. Paul was never anything but realistic, and this is probably what he had in mind in saying 'his interests are divided' (v. 34a).

What has just been said can easily give the impression that Paul glorifies the single state, and this appears to be reinforced by a number of statements in v. 32-35. To keep a sense of perspective we have to remember he also said 'Are you bound to a wife? Do not seek to be free' (v. 27a). In the framework of his temporal expectations and the real conditions of the Corinthian community Paul is against change of social status, and his point is simply that under these conditions one would be a fool to get married. It is highly likely, moreover, that the statement 'the unmarried man/woman/virgin is anxious about the affairs of the Lord' (v. 32, 34), which at first sight appears incredibly naive, is a subtle criticism of the ascetics who were creating all the trouble. If Paul says 'I want you to be free from anxieties' (v. 32a) we are not entitled to assume that he approves of the 'anxiety' of the single person, even if this has the Lord as object. The very term suggest a worried care which is out of harmony with the peace to which God calls the believer (7:15b).

Such care is rather characteristic of fallen humanity which is not conscious of God's love. In this perspective the phrase 'to please the Lord' (v. 32) appears to carry a pejorative connotation; it suggests a fawning servility whose major concern is external appearances. This interpretation is confirmed by the importance that the ascetics gave to the social situation of individuals.

In the last analysis, therefore, it is very hard to accuse Paul of glorifying the single state. It was his own, and he thought it the best (7:7), but he certainly did not make it mandatory for others (v. 35). He does in fact invoke his authority in this section but then his motive is to alleviate a burden. He authoritatively states 'if you marry you do not sin, and if a girl marries she does not sin' (v. 28), and he applies this judgment to the situation of widows (v. 39) but specially to a spiritual marriage in v. 36 (where 'his betrothed' is literally 'his virgin'). Even though these have made a vow or promise of celibacy in marriage, if they cannot control their sex-drive they should enter into a normal married relationship without any scruple. The key phrase here is 'it has to be' which should be interpreted in the light of 7:7b; a physical gift reveals the divine intention for that individual. A foolish decision must be revoked when God's will is perceived. It must be noted that Paul is not objecting to spiritual marriages as such. This is clear from v. 37. It may be the will of God for some, and then they have Paul's blessing.

In all this, Paul's fundamental objection is to the presumption of those who claim to know what is best for others. They could be complacent because they were concerned only with principles, and the principle in this instance may have been Jesus' statement 'If anyone comes to me and does not hate his own father and mother *and wife* and children... he cannot be my disciple' (Lk 14:26). This may be why Paul says coldly '*I* have no command of the Lord concerning virgins' (v. 25). He was well aware that the will of God regarding non-essentials could be manifested in all sorts of mysterious ways and, in consequence, believed that one had to be attentive to the concrete realities of individual lives. His basic difference from the Corinthians was that he respected the complexity of real life more than they. His judgments are based on his experience, and he was prepared to stand on that. But in order that his opinion, which he hoped would be for their benefit and the promotion of peace (v. 35), be given due attention, he reminds them, with extraordinary mildness, that he is the one entrusted by God with the care of the community (v. 25), and concludes with the massive understatement 'I think that I have the spirit of God' (v. 40). The ascetics at Corinth could have done with an equally enduring sense of humour.

2. Problems Arising from the Pagan Environment
8:1-11:1

The formulation of 8:1 highlights the transition to another point in the letter from the Corinthians to Paul. The problem is now the legitimacy of eating meat which had been offered to idols. A proportion of the meat of animals offered in sacrifice in pagan temples became the property of the priests (9:13). They supplemented their income by selling, in the open market, what they did not need for their own use. The Christians at Corinth were divided on the morality of eating such meat. The Strong saw no problem, but the Weak felt it to be against their conscience. In 8:13 Paul argues the side of the Weak against the Strong, but when he returns to the same topic in 10:23-11:1 he feels obliged to correct the uncharitable assumption of the Weak that the Strong were acting in bad faith.

The center section (9:1-10:22) contains no direct reference to the eating of idol-meats. Thus, we have another instance of the A-B-A' pattern found previously in chs. 5, 6 and 7. The function of 9:1-10:22, however, is identical with that of 7:17-24, because there Paul deepens our understanding of the principles underlying his more practical discussions in 8:1-13 and 10:23-11:1.

The concrete problem which occasioned this section is of very limited interest, but the way in which the issue was raised forced Paul to deal with such fundamental questions as the nature of christian freedom, the place of a believer in a non-christian society, and the education of conscience. These are still living questions, and his principles are of perennial value.

THE DELICACY WITH WHICH THEORY MUST BE PUT INTO PRACTICE.
8:1-13.

8 Now concerning food offered to idols; we know that "all of us possess knowledge." "Knowledge" puffs up, but love builds up. ²If any one imagines that he knows something he does not yet know as he ought to know. ³But if one loves God, one is known by him.

⁴Hence, as to the eating of food offered to idols, we know that "an idol has no real existence," and that "there is no God but one." ⁵For although there may be so-called gods in heaven or on earth—as indeed there are many "gods" and many "lords"—⁶yet for us there is one God, the Father, from whom are all things and for whom we exist, and one Lord, Jesus Christ, through whom are all things and through whom we exist.

⁷However, not all possess this knowledge. But some, through being hitherto accustomed to idols, eat food as really offered to an idol; and their conscience, being weak,

is defiled. [8]Food will not commend us to God. We are no worse off if we do not eat, and no better off if we do. [9]Only take care lest this liberty of yours somehow becomes a stumbling block to the weak. [10]For if any one sees you, a man of knowledge, at table in an idol's temple, might he not be encouraged, if his conscience is weak, to eat food offered to idols? [11]And so by your knowledge this weak man is destroyed, the brother for whom Christ died. [12]Thus, sinning against your brethren and wounding their conscience when it is weak, you sin against Christ. [13]Therefore, if food is a cause of my brother's falling, I will never eat meat, lest I cause my brother to fall.

This chapter provides a very happy contrast to the previous one, because here we have very detailed information on the position of the Strong. Not only does Paul quote three of their statements (v. 1, 4, 8), he also mentions one thing they did (v. 10). It is much easier, therefore, to determine precisely what Paul was trying to say.

In view of what we have learned regarding the attitude, of at least some at Corinth, to the body (see on 6:12-20) it is highly unlikely that the Strong saw any problem in the eating of meat offered to idols. If every physical action was morally irrelevant, no questions were to be asked regarding any menu. It became a problem only when the Weak attacked them. The statements of the Strong in v. 1, 4, and 8 were formulated to prove that the criticism of the Weak was inconsistent with their principles.

The Strong started by affirming 'all of us possess knowledge' (v. 1). Knowledge shared by all the members of the community must concern something basic to christian belief, and what this is appears in the two statements in inverted commas in v. 4. In being converted the Weak must have accepted the belief that there was only one true God (1 Thess 1:9; Acts 14:15). In consequence, the character of meat offered to non-existent 'gods' was not changed in any way. The argument concludes in v. 8 which should be set in inverted commas and translated as follows: 'Food will not bring us before the judgment-seat of God. We are neither better off if we do not eat, nor worse off if we do.' The Weak had threatened the Strong with the wrath of God. The latter reply that, if all food comes from the one true God, there is no danger of their being brought before him for judgment (v. 8a). To justify this confidence they shift to the present tense in v. 8bc and propose a concrete criterion. All the Corinthians attached great importance to 'spiritual gifts' (chs. 12-14). Since these came from God (12:6) they could be used as a test of one's standing before God. It is unreasonable to suppose (the Strong argued) that he would give such gifts to those who displeased him; on the contrary he would be more likely to withdraw them. Just look at the facts (say the Strong). Those who refuse to eat idol-meats show no evidence of any increase in their gifts, and those who eat such meat experience no diminution in their gifts (v. 8bc).

In consequence, the Strong, having demolished the position of the Weak, continued to eat idol-meats, and even participated in banquets in pagan temples where such meat was served as a matter of course (v. 10a), and insisted to Paul that 'the weak conscience (of those who opposed them) should be built-up to the point where they could eat idol-meats without scruples' (v. 10b).

In his response Paul takes up each of these points in turn. He agrees with the Strong that there is nothing wrong with eating idol-meats (10:19, 25, 27), but he finds that they have failed to give due importance to critical aspects both of their own existence and of that of the Weak. The issue was clear to them only because they over-simplified.

The most fundamental element that the Strong found convenient to ignore was the fact that they were Christians! Their argument was based on purely theistic principles (v. 4, 8). Hence, he has to remind them of who they are, because only then could they 'know as they ought to know' (v. 2b). God had not chosen them because they were intelligent. He had known them (v. 3; Rom 8:29) long before they knew him, and the effect of his discerning knowledge was to place them in the category of 'those who love God' (v. 3; 2:9; Rom 8:28). If their new being is constituted by love (13:2; 2 Cor 5:17), every act of intelligence must be rooted in a love which discerns the real situation of the other. This provides the framework in which Paul takes up the two Corinthian statements in v. 4.

The Weak had certainly subscribed to the view that 'an idol has no real existence' (v. 4), but Paul has to remind the Strong of the difference between theoretical acceptance and emotional assimilation. The Weak mouthed the words but in their hearts they were still influenced by the conditioning of decades (v. 7), and emotionally they held the 'gods' of their past in awe. These remained 'gods' for those who believed in them, and the reality of this emotional link was not destroyed by the simple affirmation that they have no real existence (v. 5). The Strong assumed that the subjective world of all believers was the same because they had professed the same truth. Paul implies that if they saw the Weak as 'brothers' (v. 11-12), and not merely as thinking beings, they would be less confident in presuming uniformity.

In order to convince the Strong that they must think of the Weak as 'brothers' Paul fills out their assertion 'there is no God but one' (v. 4) by the famous lapidary statement of v. 6. The Greek here has no verbs, and we come closer to Paul's meaning if (in opposition to the RSV) we supply verbs of movement rather than the static 'are' and 'exist': 'For us (there is) one God, the Father, from whom (come) all things and towards whom (we go), and one Lord, Jesus Christ, by whom (come) all things and by whom we (go).' This statement is in fact an acclamation uttered during a baptismal liturgy where the saving power of God was most dramatically displayed and intensely experienced. It is cited by Paul in the hope that it will function as an emotional trigger which will revive in the Strong the memories of their own baptism. They are what they are because of the grace mediated through baptism, and this grace is the grace of Christ. In consequence, their relation to God is mediated by

Christ, and theoretical speculation on the divinity must yield to the challenge of an historical personality who is 'the power of God and the wisdom of God' (1:24). Most importantly, their baptism was a rite of initiation into a community (12:13). They had chosen to belong, and in all practical judgments they must be conscious of the interpersonal responsibility they thereby assumed.

It is hardly surprising, therefore, that Paul simply ignores the criterion proposed by the Strong in v. 8, and instead substitutes the only adequate criterion for a Christian: will this injure someone weaker than I? (v. 9). Judged against this standard the Strong certainly appeared worthy of divine condemnation when we visualise the type of pressure their behaviour brought to bear on the Weak (v. 10).

At Corinth the ex-pagans in the community had friends and relatives who had not become christian, and Paul did not forbid association with them (5:10). Marriages and funerals normally involved meals in the temple precincts, and participation in such meals, at which food offered to idols was served, was a matter of family and/or social duty. The fact that the Strong took part in such affairs (v. 10) put the Weak in a most invidious position. They were revolted by the thought of eating idol-meats (v. 7), possibly because they feared that it would once again bring them within the sphere of influence of 'gods' whom they had repudiated. Yet they could not justify their reluctance to particpate on the grounds that they were now Christians, because other believers had no such scruples. Hence, they were forced to choose between following their instincts or giving the impression that they wanted to have nothing more to do with well-loved family or friends. They could not do the latter, and so were compelled to eat meat which revolted them.

The arguments of the Strong did not touch the Weak, but the social pressure generated by the former was another matter. It effectively touched the Weak on the emotional level which is precisely where the problem lay, but it did not solve the emotional tension under which the Weak lived. It simply forced them to suppress one of the stress elements and this inevitably provoked the pain of 'conscience'. Paul rightly emphasises the destructive effect of such repression (v. 11). Those whom Christ had made whole are again torn and divided within themselves.

But the consequences were much more serious than that, for to sin against a brother is to 'sin against Christ' (v. 12). 'Christ' here means the community, as in 6:15 and 12:12, and this dimension is formally underlined by the shift from 'brother' (v. 11, 13) to 'brothers'. A sin against one member was a sin again all (5:6; 2 Cor 2:5). To destroy one was to sunder the bonds of love (Col 3:14) on which all depended (13:2). By their arrogance the Strong brought the whole community to the brink of ruin, and thus endangered the saving presence of Christ in the world (see on 6:15), and tended to negate the effectiveness of his saving death. By acting without love the Strong were in the process of dissolving the unity which was the basis of their new being. In destroying the Weak they were destroying themselves.

It is noteworthy that nowhere in this chapter does Paul tell the Strong what to do. He simply highlights those aspects of the problem which they had passed over in silence, and draws attention to the implications of their position. This is typical of his pedagogical approach which is designed to enable others to grow. The Strong had tried to force-feed the 'conscience' of the Weak with knowledge. Paul did not believe that conscience could be educated by such direct methods since emotional factors were such an important component. In consequence, he does not try to bully the consciences of the Strong by intellectual arguments. He contents himself with setting up the real situation so clearly that they can draw the correct conclusions for themselves. And in order to make his point inescapable he passionately articulates what he himself would do under similar circumstances (v. 13). He consistently avoids anything (however legitimate it may be in itself) if it is likely to create an insupportable burden for a weaker brother.

PAUL RENOUNCES HIS OWN RIGHTS
9:1-27.

9 Am I not free? Am I not an apostle? Have I not seen Jesus our Lord? Are not you my workmanship in the Lord? ²If to others I am not an apostle, at least I am to you; for you are the seal of my apostleship in the Lord.

³This is my defense to those who would examine me. ⁴Do we not have the right to our food and drink? ⁵Do we not have the right to be accompanied by a wife, as the other apostles and the brothers of the Lord and Cephas? ⁶Or is it only Barnabas and I who have no right to refrain from working for a living? ⁷Who serves as a soldier at his own expense? Who plants a vineyard without eating any of its fruit? Who tends a flock without getting some of the milk?

⁸Do I say this on human authority? Does not the law say the same? ⁹For it is written in the law of Moses, "You shall not muzzle an ox when it is treading out the grain." Is it for oxen that God is concerned? ¹⁰Does he not speak entirely for our sake? It was written for our sake, because the plowman should plow in hope and the thresher thresh in hope of a share in the crop. ¹¹If we have sown spiritual good among you, is it too much if we reap your material benefits? ¹²If others share this rightful claim upon you, do not we still more?

Nevertheless, we have not made use of this right, but we endure anything rather than put an obstacle in the way of the gospel of Christ. ¹³Do you not know that those who are employed in the temple service get their food from the temple, and those who serve at the altar share in the sacrificial offerings? ¹⁴In the same way, the Lord commanded that those who proclaim the gospel should get their living by the gospel.

¹⁵But I have made no use of any of these rights, nor am I writing this to secure any such provision. For I would rather die than have any one deprive me of my ground for boasting. ¹⁶For if I preach the gospel, that gives me no

ground for boasting. For necessity is laid upon me. Woe
to me if I do not preach the gospel! [17]For if I do this of my
own will, I am entrusted with a commission. [18]What then
is my reward? Just this: that in my preaching I may make
the gospel free of charge, not making full use of my right
in the gospel.

[19]For though I am free from all men, I have made
myself a slave to all, that I might win the more. [20]To the
Jews I became as a Jew, in order to win Jews; to those
under the law I became as one under the law—though not
being myself under the law—that I might win those under
the law. [21]To those outside the law I became as one outside
the law—not being without law toward God but under the
law of Christ—that I might win those outside the law.
[22]To the weak I became weak, that I might win the weak.
I have become all things to all men, that I might by
all means save some. [23]I do it all for the sake of the gospel,
that I may share in its blessings.

[24]Do you not know that in a race all the runners
compete, but only one receives the prize? So run that you
may obtain it. [25]Every athlete exercises self-control in all
things. They do it to receive a perishable wreath, but we an
imperishable. [26]Well, I do not run aimlessly, I do not box
as one beating the air; [27]but I pommel my body and
subdue it, lest after preaching to others I myself should be
disqualified

Paul has just been asking the Strong to freely renounce
their right to eat idol-meat because this is demanded by the
needs of weaker brethren. He repudiated the tendency of the
Strong to think of things 'in themselves'; everything must be
viewed within the concrete framework of present circumstances. He was not sure, however, that this would win
immediate acceptance, probably because he had received
some indications that his own behaviour had come under
criticism at Corinth (v. 3); he accepted restrictions on
his own freedom which were not shared by other apostles.
Such self-imposed restrictions were, in Paul's eyes, an

integral part of the christian life, so evident that he had never thought of justifying them. With their genius for misinterpretation some at Corinth saw Paul's non-use of certain rights as evidence that he was not really an apostle. 'If he really is an apostle,' they argued, 'he should demand that we support him financially, as we do other apostles (v. 12). If he does not demand such support, it is because he has no right to it. Therefore he is not an apostle.' Such an attitude explains the passionate character of Paul's response, and he deals with it at this point in the letter because his own behaviour (when properly understood) furnishes a perfect example of what he has been trying to convey to the Strong.

The two topics dealt with in this chapter are spelled out in the questions 'Am I not free? Am I not an apostle?' (v. 1a). These are taken up in turn but in inverse order. The question of Paul's apostolic authority occupies v. 1b-18, and his understanding of his freedom appears in v. 19-27.

Paul fulfils one of the criteria by which an apostle is judged because he saw the Risen Lord (v. 1b). The reference is to his experience on the Damascus Road (Acts 9:1-18; 22:5-16; 26:9-18; Gal 1:12-17; 1 Cor 15:8). The ability to bear first-hand witness to the fact of the resurrection was the indispensable foundation of apostleship in the strict sense (Acts 1:22). However, not all those who had seen the Lord after the resurrection became apostles, but only those who had received a commission to preach. How could the Corinthians know that Paul had received such a commission. The simple answer that Paul provides is the fact that every effect presupposes a cause. The mere existence of the community at Corinth proves that Paul enjoys a power deriving from Christ (v. 2; 2 Cor 3:2-3). They had experienced this power. They do not have to take it on faith. They were the last people who should question his authority. It is easy to see that Paul is cut to the quick.

This being the case, Paul continues, I have all the rights of an apostle (v. 4-5). The RSV version of v. 5a is a possible translation of the Greek, but it is more likely that the

meaning is 'Have we not the right to be married?' The
mention of women at this point is curious because marriage
plays no role in the subsequent discussion, and the most
reasonable explanation for its inclusion is that Paul was led
astray by a popular association of ideas suggested by the
(very relevant) mention of eating and drinking (v. 4). These
are the first two of a triad 'to eat, drink, and be merry', the
last term being a euphemism for sexual intercourse (10:7; 2
Sm 11:11; Ex 32:6; Lk 12:19). Paul was certainly single at
this time (7:7), but there is no way of knowing whether he
was a widower or a bachelor.

The right to be married was much less important (given
the concrete circumstances of Paul's relation with the
Corinthians) than the 'right not to have to work for a living'
(v. 6), because Paul goes on to produce a series of arguments
designed to show that an apostle does not have to have a
trade in order to provide the revenue which will enable him
to eat, drink, and support a wife. There are four arguments,
and each pair (v. 7-12a and 13-14) is followed by Paul's
assertion that he has not used this right (v. 12b and 15-18).

The first two arguments are based on commonsense (v. 7-
8a) and on the Law of Moses (v. 9-12a). Paul's exegesis of Dt
25:4 may seem forced, but it is a simple argument from the
lesser to the greater which was widely used to defend the
principle of a fair return for a workman's labor. If God
shows such concern for the sustenance of working beasts, he
must have intended that those who labor in his service
should be able to live from what they do for him. The right
to reward is founded on service, not on position, and Paul
has certainly rendered service to the Corinthians (v. 11). His
keep is a small return for the privilege of having had the
gospel preached to them, and the Corinthians must
recognise the force of this argument because they had
supported others who had contributed less (v. 12a).

The second pair of arguments are drawn from the practice
of both Jewish and pagan temples (v. 13) and from a
command of Jesus (v. 14). The RSV translation of v. 14
gives the impression that it is addressed to the community. In

fact it reads, 'The Lord commanded those who proclaim the gospel to get their living by the gospel'. It imposes an obligation on the preachers to accept support. Paul must be alluding to passages such as Mt 10:7-14 and Lk 10:3-11, but his version does not agree either in letter or in spirit with that of the gospels. The basic thrust of these latter is: don't ask for money, trust in providence! The implication of the Pauline version is that the Lord desired only full-time preachers. They were not to devote precious time to earning their own living.

It is obvious that this last argument (v. 14) is quite different from the other three. These establish the existence of a 'right', i.e. a discretionary privilege which the beneficiary is entitled to renounce. The command of the Lord, on the contrary, imposes an 'obligation'. One cannot simply waive an obligation. It can only be obeyed or disobeyed. This puts Paul's refusal to accept support in a very different light, and we are forced to ask by what authority he reclassified an 'obligation' as a 'right'.

This is not an isolated incident, because Paul exhibits the same reaction to the commandment concerning divorce (see on 7:15). His practice shows conclusively that he considered the commands of Jesus, not as binding precepts, but as guidelines to be used critically (1 Thess 5:21). His respect for the value of the guideline is proven by the fact that he quotes it even when he intends to do the opposite, but the ultimate criterion on which Paul relies is his own assessment of the concrete situation. In the present case he refuses to obey because he felt that to accept money for preaching might 'put an obstacle in the way of the gospel of Christ' (v. 12b).

It is easy to imagine what Paul has in mind. He gives tremendous importance to existential witness in which the prime factor is the conviction of the believer. To accept money for preaching could give the impression that it was just a job (2 Cor 2:17), and could inspire envy because talking is not the most exhausting form of work. By preaching at his own expense (1 Thess 2:9) Paul hoped that the strength of his conviction would become apparent (v.

1b; 2 Cor 5:14). On another level, Paul could not permit the question of support to determine the places in which he preached. Was the gospel to be denied to those too poor to support an apostle? Was he to limit his apostolate to those rich enough to provide food and drink? Paul was also aware that prospective converts might hesitate if they saw that acceptance of the gospel also involved a financial commitment to support a pastor. Paul rightly felt that reasons such as these justified his disobedience to the command of the Lord, and he perhaps remembered that the same Lord had also said 'freely you have received, freely give' (Mt 10:8b).

Paul is proud of his financial independence (v. 15). He has made no use of the 'reasons' (not 'rights' as in RSV), i.e. the four arguments, which could justify a claim to be supported at the expense of the community, and he does not intend to do so now. This was only partially true, and Paul got into serious trouble when the Corinthians discovered his misrepresentation. While at Corinth he had been receiving money from other churches (2 Cor 11:7-9; 12:11-16). Similarly, he had told the Thessalonians that he earned his own living (1 Thess 2:6-9), even though he was in receipt of aid from Philippi (Phil 4:15-16). From these two instances we can infer that it was Paul's practice to accept support from a community *only after he had left it.* He took nothing from the community in which he was actually working.

His words (v. 15-18) give a different impression, and it is unpleasant to read them when one is aware of the underlying mental reservation. We must, however, respect Paul's insistence that he preaches the gospel because he believes that he has no choice. He feels compelled to proclaim the good news (v. 16). If he freely chose to preach, he could expect a reward, but this is not in fact the case. He did not choose to be an apostle. He was entrusted with a commission which left him with no option (v. 17). Here, we get a redeeming touch of humor, 'What are the wages of one who is not entitled to any? Why, to do the work for free!' (v. 18), which is immediately countered by a subtle safeguard because Paul says that he does not make *'full* use of my right in the gospel' (v. 18). This is the truth, because he was making *some* use of his right to support, and provides the necessary corrective to the previous exaggeration.

Even though Paul received aid from other churches, it is impossible to say whether he really needed it or not. Certainly, there is no hint that he asked for it, and the only satisfactory explanation of v. 19 is based on the assumption that Paul felt himself perfectly capable of providing for himself. Being beholden to no one for his livelihood, he is not subject to the pressures which enslave those who are financially dependent. He is 'free from all men' (v. 19), and so he could afford to ignore them. Because of the strength of their conviction the Strong found themselves in the same position, but whereas they tried to preserve the sensation of being free by acting in such a way as to demonstrate their independence, Paul makes himself 'the slave of all' (v. 19). The lesson to the Strong is clear, and is forced home as Paul emphasises the sacrifices he makes in order to win men to Christ. Far from being lost, his freedom is affirmed in renunciation.

Paul surrenders his personal inclinations in order to insert himself into a series of groups: the Jews, those under the Law, the Law-less, and the Weak (v. 20-22a). Even though repetition in such a short list is unusual, the first two groups are identical. Paul started off to write Jews and Greeks, a frequent formula in his letters (1:24; 10:32; 12:13; Rom 1:16; 2:9; 3:9; 10:12; Gal 3:28), but having written 'Jews', he saw the advantage of bringing in a reference to the Law, because the slogan of the Strong, 'all things are lawful to me' (6:12; 10:23) showed that they were 'law-less'. Hence, he redefined 'Jews' as 'those under the Law' because this permitted him to introduce the polyvalent 'Law-less' which, on the one hand, means gentiles (Rom 2:14), but which, on the other hand, could refer to the lawless Strong. This subtle shift makes the movement to v. 22a entirely natural because he would have instinctively associated the 'Weak' with the Strong.

When among Jews, Paul behaved as a Jew both socially and religiously (v. 20). This gave him an entree which he would not otherwise have had. In all this context Paul's principle is 'Become as I am because I became as you' (Gal 4:12). The preacher must be integrated to the point where he can command a sympathetic hearing. There must be nothing in his bearing or attitudes which would induce his prospective audience to reject him out of hand. Paul, therefore, when with Jews conformed his behaviour to the directives of the Law of Moses. He, however, is concerned to emphasise formally that he did not consider himself to be bound by that Law. This is one of the most radical statements in his letters, because if the Law of Moses is no longer binding, all positive law is repudiated. The Christian cannot regulate his life by obedience to precepts, and Paul lives this in his attitude to the precepts of Jesus (see on 7:15 and 9:14).

Among Gentiles Paul lives as if he had never heard of the Law, but his behaviour was not governed by subjective caprice. He refuses to submit to a 'thing', a written code, but he does submit to a 'person', namely, God (v. 21). The RSV translation 'law toward God' is meaningless. The Greek is simply 'the law of God', and the genitive here (in the light of v. 20) can only be explicative, 'the law which is God'. What guides Paul is the divine intention for humanity. But where is this manifested? In Christ. Hence, for all practical purposes Paul is guided by 'the law which is Christ' and whose single demand is love (Gal 6:2). The relevance of this point to the situation of the Strong hardly needs emphasis. The other, not self, must be the center of their concern.

The Weak are, in the first place, the scrupulous brethren who were the object of Paul's solicitude in ch. 8, but it would be wrong to exclude all others who labor under any sort of weakness. With these Paul identifies completely; note the absence of any 'as' (v. 20-21) in 'I became weak' (v. 22a). He consistently emphasises that his apostolate is characterised by 'weakness'. It was this transparency which permitted the power of God to shine through, 'We have this power in earthen vessels, to show that the transcendent power belongs to God and not to us' (2 Cor 4:7; cf. 1 Cor 1:23; 4:10; 2 Cor 10:10; 11:21-30; 12:9-10; 13:9; Gal 4:13). The form of Paul's weakness obviously differed from that of the Weak, but there was a real parallel when viewed in terms of the ideal. Equally, 'win' does not have exactly the same meaning here, where Paul has Christians in mind, as it does in v. 20-21, where he is thinking of making converts. The difference should not be exaggerated, however, because Paul never thinks of conversion as an end itself. It is but the first step in a process which will culminate only on the day of the Lord. Each individual has to be continually 're-won' for Christ. Growth in Christ is essentially a series of new and deeper conversions. Paul takes up this theme again in v. 24-27.

Integrity is normally defined as being true to oneself. How then can Paul be 'all things to all men' (v. 22b)? Only by finding a point of reference outside himself; the basis of genuine christian integrity is commitment to the truth of the gospel (v. 23). If a subjective self-image (with consistency as the main ingredient) is made the criterion, adaptation can be only superficial, and witness is vitiated by an element of fake. Even idiots recognize condescension. Since Paul's christian and apostolic vocations are but two facets of the same reality, he has to surrender all in order to win others to Christ. As an apostle he can be saved only through saving others; his reward is to be 'a co-sharer in the blessings of the gospel' (v. 23).

This hint of the possibility of failure brings Paul's attention back to the Corinthians. They tended to see their conversion as the achievement of a perfect and indefectible state, whereas for Paul it was only the recovery of a freedom which might be used as an opportunity for growth or lost through abuse. Hence, he has to remind them that entry in a competition does not in itself guarantee a prize (v. 24), and that no success is possible in any race without consistent effort (v. 25). The athlete rigorously excludes everything that would interfere with the achievement of his object, and believers must do the same. By switching back to the first person singular Paul tactfully conveys his conviction that the Strong do not really know where they are going (v. 26). He knows where he is going because he has a clear vision of the ideal towards which he strives, and he drags in a reference to the body, not because asceticism has a value in itself, but because of the Corinthian conviction that the body did not matter (v. 27). Paul's concern is not with the body as such (he never thinks of anything 'as such') but with the body as the instrument of commitment. Behaviour patterns owe as much to physical preconditioning as they do to mental attitudes. Hence, for those coming from the egocentric 'world', a repressive stance with regard to the body is just as necessary as conversion of mind and heart. The inherited 'desires of the flesh' are not silenced by a contrary intention (Gal 5:1-26).

THE DANGERS OF OVER-CONFIDENCE.
10:1-13.

10   I want you to know, brethren, that our fathers were all under the cloud, and all passed through the sea, ²and all were baptized into Moses in the cloud and in the sea, ³and all ate the same supernatural food ⁴and all drank the same supernatural drink. For they drank from the supernatural Rock which followed them, and the Rock was Christ. ⁵Nevertheless with most of them God was not pleased; for they were overthrown in the wilderness.

⁶Now these things are warnings for us, not to desire evil as they did. ⁷Do not be idolaters as some of them were; as it is written. "The people sat down to eat and drink and rose up to dance." ⁸We must not indulge in immorality as some of them did, and twenty-three thousand fell in a single day. ⁹We must not put the Lord to the test, as some of them did and were destroyed by serpents; ¹⁰nor grumble, as some of them did and were destroyed by the Destroyer. ¹¹Now these things happened to them as a warning, but they were written down for our instruction,

upon whom the end of the ages has come. [12]Therefore let any one who thinks that he stands take heed lest he fall. [13]No temptation has overtaken you that is not common to man. God is faithful, and he will not let you be tempted beyond your strength, but with the temptation will also provide the way of escape, that you may be able to endure it.

Even though he seems to have wandered far from the question of idol-meats (ch. 8) Paul has not really lost sight of it at all. The Strong should have refrained from something good in itself out of deference to the weakness of some members of the community. In order to illustrate what he has in mind Paul proposes the example of his own behaviour (ch. 9). But the Strong acted as they did because the strength of their conviction gave them a sense of unshakable security, and because they felt their motives to be pure and their physical actions to be morally irrelevant (see on 6:12-20). Paul now turns his attention to the task of breaking down this sense of complacent superiority which was the psychological obstacle to their following his directives. The basic message he wants to get across is, 'Let anyone who thinks he stands take heed lest he fall' (v. 12) and the means he uses is a lesson from the history of salvation. He shows that there is a parallel between the situation of the Israelites in the desert and that of the Strong at Corinth. Hence, what happened to the Israelites could also happen to the Strong.

Paul takes it for granted that his readers are familiar with the Exodus narrative. We have to assume, therefore, that the gentiles who made up the majority of the community at Corinth (Acts 18:4, 7) had either been converts to Judaism, or at least belonged to the group of the 'God-fearers' (Acts 13:16, 26) who had been exposed to Jewish instruction (see on 2:6-3:4). The major episodes of the desert journey are mentioned in the same order in which they appear in the book of Exodus: the cloud (Ex 13:21), the sea (Ex 14:21), the manna (Ex 16:4, 14-18), the water from the rock (Ex 17:6), and the rebellion (Ex 32:6). These episodes were known to Paul and his readers, not as bald texts of the Old Testament, but as elements of a living interpretative tradition which modified details, furnished explanations, and made applications. Unless this is recognised it is difficult to see how Paul is justified in handling the OT as he does.

Paul's purpose in v. 1-2 is to force the Strong to see a parallel between the Israelites passing through the sea under the cloud, and christian baptism. He was enabled to see this link because his Jewish contemporaries obliged converts to Judaism to undergo a form of baptism (proselyte baptism), and sought justification for this in the passage of their people through the sea. Given this, it was almost inevitable that the cloud, which represented divine protection and guidance, and the sea, which saved the Israelites from Egyptian pursuit, should be seen as symbols of the Spirit and water in baptism. Hence, Paul speaks of a 'baptism into Moses' (v. 2). There are no Jewish parallels to this formula which Paul invented with the intention that the Strong should think of their own 'baptism into Christ' (Rom 6:3; Gal 3:27). It is excellent pedagogy to set things up so that readers think the conclusion to be their own.

Paul then evokes the manna and the water from the rock which God miraculously provided to sustain the Israelites, but instead of using the terms 'manna' and 'water' he speaks of 'spiritual food' and 'spiritual drink' (v. 3-4: change 'supernatural' of RSV). This legitimate generalisation was designed to enable anyone who had perceived the allusion to baptism in v. 1-2 to see here a reference to the eucharist. There is no question of logical necessity. Paul relies on an instinctive association of ideas in the minds of those familiar with the components of the eucharist (11:26; *Didache* 10:3).

Passages such as Pss 78:20; 105:41; Is 48:21 provide a basis for the legend that a stream of water followed the Israelites in the desert. The well of Num 21: 7-18 was also considered to have moved with them, and this latter legend is attested about the time of Paul (Pseudo-Philo 10:7). Very late Jewish sources say that the moving well was in the shape of a rock, but it is nowhere called a rock as in v. 4b. This half-verse does not fit easily into Paul's presentation here (a reference to the Cephas party parallel to 3:11 appears excluded by the nature of the context). In particular the function of the causal particle 'for' is far from clear, since the adjective 'spiritual' could have been applied to the manna and the water independently of any reference to the 'rock' (Ps 78:25; Wis 16:20; Ex 17:6), and in fact the 'spiritual food' is not given any causal foundation. Moreover, the absence of 'all' breaks the pattern of v. 1-4a. Finally, the basis of typology is not the pre-existence of Christ (which here cannot be interpreted as meaning existence before creation) but the fact that the one God is the master of all history. Hence the possibility that v. 4b is a post-Pauline gloss should be given serious consideration.

Having shown the Strong that 'all' who were in the desert enjoyed gifts similar to baptism and the eucharist, Paul immediately introduces his main point 'with most of them God was not pleased' (v. 5). The privileges they enjoyed did not guarantee their security. Of all those who had left Egypt only two entered the promised land, the rest having perished in punishment (Num 14:16, 30-32). All that happened in the desert were 'types' (not 'warnings' as in RSV). Some were good (gifts) and some were bad (punishment). Knowing that they have received good things from God (baptism and eucharist) the Strong should be aware that they will also receive bad unless they cease 'to desire evil as they did' (v. 6).

This desire for evil things is broken down by Paul into four specific sins: idolatry (v. 7), immorality (v. 8), testing God (v. 9), and grumbling (v. 10). All are solidly rooted in the Exodus narrative, but we must assume that Paul mentions them in detail because of their relevance to the Corinthian situation. The complacent superiority of the Strong tested God because it amounted to rejection of the conditions of the New Covenant. Their immorality is evident in 5:1-5 and 6:12-20, and hints of their grumbling were detected in ch. 9. If they did not worship false gods, they gave the impression they did (8:10; 10:14-22). What happened to the Israelites who did these things is well documented, and this is evidence of God's mercy because it was written down so that similar mistakes could be avoided in the future (v. 11; Rom 15:4). Would that the 'wise' would look squarely at the factual evidence of the way God deals with humanity (v. 12), and benefit by the accumulated experience of all completed ages (v. 11b).

In a switch of position that is psychologically very effective Paul then informs the Strong that the tests, which they have failed, are the common lot of humanity (v. 13a). Their 'wisdom' did not permit them to see the pitfalls into which every Tom, Dick, and Harry tumbles. The future, however, will bring something different, and it is likely that Paul is here thinking of the great period of trial that will precede the end (7:26, 29). Then the Strong will have to be specially careful, but they can take consolation from the fact that God will never permit them to be tested in such a way that failure is inevitable (v. 13b).

THE SIGNIFICANCE OF SOCIAL GESTURES. 10:14-22.

> [14]Therefore, my beloved, shun the worship of idols. [15]I speak as to sensible men; judge for yourselves what I say. [16]The cup of blessing which we bless, is it not a participation in the body of Christ? [17]Because there is one bread, we who are many are one body, for we all partake of the one bread. [18]Consider the practice of Israel; are not those who eat the sacrifices partners in the altar? [19]What do I imply then? That food offered to idols is anything, or that an idol is anything? [20]No, I imply that what pagans sacrifice they offer to demons and not to God, I do not want you to be partners with demons. [21]You cannot drink the cup of the Lord and the cup of demons. You cannot partake of the table of the Lord and the table of demons. [22]Shall we provoke the Lord to jealousy? Are we stronger than he?

In the previous section Paul had said 'Do not be idolaters' (v. 7), but this demanded clarification because the Strong maintained that 'an idol has no real existence' (8:4). They knew that pagan rituals had lost all meaning and value. Hence, for them participation in temple banquets (8:10) were simply social occasions which carried no negative implications regarding their commitment to Christ. They had no intention of worshipping idols. Paul, however, believed that social gestures had an objective significance which was independent of the intention of those who made them. We have seen him work this out with regard to the act of sexual intercourse (6:12-20). Just as there he said 'Shun immorality" (6:18a), so here he insists 'Shun the worship of idols' (v. 14). His position on both issues is fundamentally the same, and so is his approach, because in both instances he appeals to the intelligence of the Strong (v. 15).

His first concern is to establish common ground with the Strong. The form of the rhetorical question 'is it not' (v. 16), which expects an affirmative answer, indicates that he has found this in the christian parallel to a pagan temple banquet, the eucharist (v. 16). He takes it for granted that the Strong admit the identification of the cup and the bread with Christ, and that they concede that their participation in the eucharistic meal produces a real effect. This effect he defines as *koinōnia* which is best translated as 'communion' (RSV 'participation') provided that this is understood as meaning 'common union', because v. 17 shows that there is a double point of reference. Through sharing in the body and blood of Christ, believers are united with him *and* with each other. The physical gesture of eating and drinking at the christian sacred meal has the effect of bringing into being a new Body which is the physical presence of Christ in the world (see on 6:15; 8:12; 12:12-27). All are united with Christ through faith and baptism (Gal 3:26-28). The physical gesture of eating and drinking adds a new dimension. Since all share in the one drink which is Christ and in the one bread which is Christ, Christ (to put it very crudely) becomes a possession which all hold in common, and are thereby forged into unity.

Having stated what he believes to be common ground, Paul looks for an analogy whose illustrative power will diminish the possibility of misunderstanding. Further evidence that the Strong (among others in the Corinthian community) had received Jewish instruction (see on 10:1-13) is provided by the fact that he appeals to the practice of 'the historical Israel' (v. 18: the RSV omits 'according to the flesh' which is here translated by 'historical'). What Paul has in mind is the 'sacrifice of communion' in which the victim was divided between God (represented by the 'altar'), the priest and the offerer (Lev 3 and 7). The part pertaining to the offerer was eaten by his family and guests in a state of ritual purity (1 Sam 9:10-24). The sacrifice is offered to God, but because the meat is shared, the implication is that God invites them to sit at table with him, and *koinōnia* is the result, a 'common union' with him and with others.

The stage is now set, and it only remains for Paul to draw the obvious conclusion. If the Strong participate in pagan temple banquets, their physical gesture brings them into a 'common union' with idols and with those who worship them. Whatever be their intention, their physical stance brings them into the category of 'idolaters' (v. 7-14).

Paul, however, does not say this because he immediately anticipates an objection of the Strong. They had denied the reality of idols (8:4), and it would be natural for them to protest that there was no analogy between the eucharist or Jewish sacrifice and pagan temple meals. Hence, Paul at once insists that the validity of the analogy does not depend on acceptance of the view that an idol is capable of efficacious action (v. 19). An idol has no real existence, and meat offered to one is not changed in any way. The analogy with the eucharist or Jewish sacrifices, therefore, breaks down on one point. For Paul, however, ritual gestures had both vertical and horizontal implications. The denial of the vertical dimension in idol-worship did not destroy the horizontal relationship established by the gesture of sharing. The Strong, therefore, entered into a 'common union' with pagans who by their belief gave idols a subjective existence which facilitated the activity of the anti-God forces at loose in the world ('demons'). The pagans worshipped (what to Paul were) the forces of evil, and by objectively uniting with pagans in their ritual, the Strong objectively entered into a 'common union' with such forces (v. 20). What Paul has in mind becomes perfectly clear if we remember the actual effect of the participation of the Strong in temple banquets (8:10-12). They destroyed the brother for whom Christ died, and they initiate the destruction of the community which is the agent of Christ's presence in the world. This was precisely the goal of the anti-God forces, and so the Strong were in a very real sense 'partners with demons' (v. 20). They never intended any such thing, but this is irrelevant in view of the real consequences of their action.

By the physical gesture of sharing in the eucharist the Strong forge a union designed to benefit others in the community of faith. By their physical gesture of sharing in pagan temple banquets they are working for the destruction of that union. Hence, they cannot do both (v. 21), and so must terminate their ritual association with pagans. If they do not, the consequences are likely to be unfortunate (v. 22), as 10: 1-13 has amply shown.

THE SCRUPLES OF THE WEAK.
10:23-11:1.

> [23]All things are lawful," but not all things are helpful. "All things are lawful," but not all things build up. [24]Let no one seek his own good, but the good of his neighbor. [25]Eat whatever is sold in the meat market without raising any question on the ground of conscience. [26]For "the earth is the Lord's, and everything in it." [27]If one of the unbelievers invites you to dinner and you are disposed to go, eat whatever is set before you without raising any question on the ground of conscience. [28](But if some one says to you, "This has been offered in sacrifice," then out of consideration for the man who informed you, and for

conscience' sake—[29]I mean his conscience, not yours—do not eat it.) For why should my liberty be determined by another man's scruples? [30]If I partake with thankfulness, why am I denounced because of that for which I give thanks?

[31]So, whether you eat or drink, or whatever you do, do all to the glory of God. [32]Give no offense to Jews or to Greeks or to the church of God, [33]just as I try to please all men in everything I do, not seeking my own advantage, but that of many, that they may be saved.

11   Be imitators of me, as I am of Christ.

Having dealt with the Strong Paul now turns his attention to the Weak. His quotation of the slogan of the Strong, 'all things are lawful' (v. 23; 6:12), serves as a transition, because the qualifications he attaches to it are equally applicable to the Weak. Their instinctive revulsion against eating idol-meat (7:7) was understandable insofar as they had not fully succeeded in internalizing the fact that idols were nothing (8:4; 10:19). To this extent Paul could sympathize with them, and we have seen how much effort he expended in trying to rectify the attitude of the Strong who were forcing them to act against their consciences (8:1-10:22). The Weak, however, were not entirely free from blame. They could do nothing directly about the instinctive reaction of their consciences, but their agressive attack on the Strong (see on 8:8) was neither 'helpful' nor 'edifying' (v. 23). Both groups were obliged by the admonition 'Let no one seek his own good, but the good of his neighbour' (v. 24).

What this directive meant to the Strong is clear in the light of the preceding sections. What it could mean to the Weak was another matter. They could claim that they were acting in the best interests of others by trying to prevent them from eating idol-meats. Paul does not make the mistake of the Strong by attempting to confront this attitude directly. He was aware that its emotional roots were not susceptible to purely rational argumentation. The instinctive refusal of the Weak could be overcome only as a by-product of the growth towards christian maturity. Hence, Paul is content to initiate a process of edification whose key-element is the loving concern that he himself shows, and which he hoped the Strong would imitate.

His first step is the extremely pragmatic one of telling the Weak that they should not go looking for trouble. Their consciences should not bother them unless they were absolutely sure that a particular piece of meat had in fact been offered to idols, and they could avoid being absolutely sure by asking no questions regarding the origin of the meat they buy (v. 25) or which is offered to them in pagan houses (v. 27). Paul's adoption of the principle 'what you don't know won't hurt you' shows how far he has moved from Judaism where ignorance was never an obstacle to culpability.

No sooner had Paul written 'eat whatever is set before you without raising any question on the ground of conscience' (v. 27) than he realized that these words would also be read by the Strong. This is precisely what they were doing, and there was the risk that they could take it as a reversal of the position he took in ch. 8. Paul, of course, did not intend his statement here to refer to meals in pagan temples; he had excluded that in 10:21. He was referring to meals in private homes belonging to pagans. But in case the Strong did not perceive the distinction, he feels obliged to introduce a parenthetical qualification (v. 28-29a) to show that he has not changed his mind. The hypothetical informant is obviously a weak Christian, and whatever the motive behind his statement, a stronger brother must 'make a practice of abstaining from eating' (v. 29a), lest the weak one be subjected to pressure to act in a way which would result in his suffering the pangs of conscience.

Although addressed to the Strong, v. 28-29a make a point that Paul hoped the Weak would take up. They had insisted that meat should be checked 'on the ground of conscience' (v. 25, 27). This way of speaking highlights the autonomy of conscience, but the Weak exaggerated this aspect. Seeing conscience as a source of pain, the Weak feared to tamper with it. They felt that it could not be changed. Paul, therefore, has to stress that the conscience belongs to the person. This is why he speaks of 'the man who informed you' and 'his conscience'. As the person grew in Christ the instinctive judgement of conscience would undergo change.

If the Strong had to restrain themselves for the sake of the Weak, a degree of restraint was also imperative for these latter. Their complaint against the Strong contained an unjustified element which, in its own way, was just as destructive as the lack of concern of the Strong. In order to stop the Weak dead in their tracks Paul resorts to a technique which he has already used in 8:13. He shifts to the first person singular in a carefully calculated burst of passion designed to shock the Weak into a realization of the enormity of their offense. 'What good does it do for my freedom to be subjected to the judgment of another's conscience?' (v. 29b, correct RSV). The Weak had ceded to the pressure generated by the Strong (see on 8:10) and had eaten idol-meat. In consequence, they suffered the pangs of conscience. They naturally blamed the Strong for this pain, and in their anger projected onto the consciences of the Strong the reaction of their own consciences. In other words, aware that they had acted against their own instructive judgment, the Weak assumed that the Strong were doing the same.

In this situation the natural reaction of the Strong (whose side Paul takes here) would be to ask, 'Why am I defamed? The fact that I give thanks to God for what I eat shows that my conscience is clear!' (v. 30). Paul does not answer the question posed in v. 29b. He is content to exclude the false, self-serving hypothesis of the Weak in the hope that they will thereby be forced to think along more productive lines.

In order to balance the negative tone of much of the discussion occasioned by the problem of eating idol-meats Paul concludes on a highly positive note by enunciating a general principle which covers the point at issue, but which is susceptible of much wider application, 'do all to the glory of God' (v. 31). Just as the perfection of an article honors its craftsman, so believers must give glory to God by being what he intends them to be, namely, a manifestation of power-in-splendour in imitation of Christ (11:1). As the physical presence of the saving Christ, the community has a responsibility to 'hold forth the word of life' (Phil 2:16) to both Jews and Greeks. It cannot satisfy this obligation if its members exhibit the same type of bitter division that characterises the 'world' (v. 32). But it is not enough that the Corinthians avoid creating stumbling-blocks, they must actively empower the conversion of Jews and Greeks as well as the continuing growth of their fellow-believers (14:3, 24, 26) - just as Paul strives to do (v. 33). Once again, Paul assumes the burden that is his duty. Christ is the criterion of authentically human behaviour. But the Corinthians had never met him, and in order to demonstrate that this ideal is not beyond the reach of humanity, Paul has to say 'Be imitators of me, as I am of Christ' (11:1). To justify the present reality of the love of God in Christ a preacher can only point to himself. Unless he manifests in his person 'the life of Jesus' (2 Cor 4:10) he has no right to speak.

3. Problems Arising in the Liturgical Assemblies.
11:2-14:40.

It is obvious from 11:2 on that Paul is dealing with topics that have no relationship to the problem of eating idol-meats, yet there is no formula introducing a new subject as in 7:1, 25; 8:1; 12:1, nor even a phrase such as 1:11 or 5:1 indicating information coming from a source other than the Corinthian letter. The benevolent tone of 11:2, however, contrasts sharply with the extremely critical tone of the rest of ch. 11, and in particular with 11:17. This forces us to postulate ironical overtones which in turn suggests that 11:2

embodies a reference to the Corinthian letter. Following on what they had to say regarding the eating of idol-meats, they may have continued, 'Even though we disagree on the question of idol-meats, on which you gave us no direction, nonetheless we remember everything you told us, and maintain the traditions just as you delivered them to us. In particular we come together for prayer and the celebration of the eucharist.' If this was in fact the case, the transition to the problems dealt with in ch. 11 would be much less abrupt to the Corinthians than it appears to us. I doubt that the Corinthian letter contained any further information or questions regarding these liturgical assemblies. It seems more likely that Paul's reaction is based on information received orally (1:11). He decided to deal with these topics here, before passing to the question of spiritual gifts in 12:1, because he had just been dealing with social occasions involving pagans (10:14-22, 27) and this made it natural to take up social occasions within the christian community.

The section concerning spiritual gifts exhibits the A-B-A' pattern previously noted in chs. 5-7, ch. 7, and chs. 9-10. The two chapters where he speaks formally of spiritual gifts (chs. 12 and 14) are separated by a chapter devoted to love (ch. 13) which is the key to the whole section.

DRESS AT LITURGICAL ASSEMBLIES.
11:2-16.

> [2]I commend you because you remember me in everything and maintain the traditions even as I have delivered them to you. [3]But I want you to understand that the head of every man is Christ, the head of a woman is her husband, and the head of Christ is God. [4]Any man who prays or prophesies with his head covered dishonors his head,[5]but any woman who prays or prophesies with her head unveiled dishonors her head—it is the same as if her head were shaven. [6]For if a woman will not veil herself, then she should cut off her hair; but if it is disgraceful for a woman to be shorn or shaven, let her wear a veil. [7]For a

man ought not to cover his head, since he is the image and glory of God, but woman is the glory of man. [8](For man was not made from woman, but woman from man. [9]Neither was man created for woman, but woman for man.) [10]That is why a woman ought to have a veil on her head, because of the angels. [11](Nevertheless, in the Lord woman is not independent of man nor man of woman; [12]for as woman was made from man, so man is now born of woman. And all things are from God.) [13]Judge for yourselves; is it proper for a woman to pray to God with her head uncovered? [14]Does not nature itself teach you that for a man to wear long hair is degrading to him, [15]but if a woman has long hair, it is her pride? For her hair is given to her for a covering. [16]If any one is disposed to be contentious, we recognize no other practice, nor do the churches of God.

This section is normally given a title suggesting that Paul is concerned only with the women in the community, e.g. 'Headdress of Women' (New American Bible); 'Women's Behaviour at Services' (Jerusalem Bible). A simple reading of the passage shows this to be false. Paul is equally concerned with men; they are not introduced simply as a foil to what he has to say about women.

The problem here is the external appearance of both men and women as they 'pray and prophesy' (v. 4, 5, 13). According to Paul, 'The one prophesying speaks to men with a view to edification and encouragement and consolation' (14:3). Prophecy is a 'sign for believers' (14:22) and it is open to all so that 'all may learn and be encouraged' (14:31). It is, therefore, a ministry of the word deriving from a profound knowledge of the mysteries of God (13:2) based on the scriptures. It would be very difficult to justify a distinction between prophecy in this sense and our contemporary liturgical homily. Much less evidence is available regarding the nature of 'prayer', but the social context established by what has been said about 'prophecy' clearly suggests that the reference is to the inspired public prayer which summed up the faith of the community and to which assent was given by the 'Amen' of the assembly (14: 16; 2 Cor 1:20). Some of the NT hymns (Phil 2:6-11; Col 1: 15-20; 1 Tim 3:16) may be typical of such prayer (Col 3:16).

Paul, therefore, takes it entirely for granted that both men and women should undertake the liturgical leadership of the community as the occasion arises. The gifts of prayer and prophecy are given by the Spirit without any discrimination based on sex and, while Paul can attempt to introduce order into the use of charisms (14:26-33), he makes no attempt to dispute the decision of God.

What then was the problem at Corinth? Ostensibly the issue is dress, but the opacity of the passage, the sudden jumps from one argument to another which give the impression of Paul shifting from one foot to another in embarassment, and the final legalistic slamming of the door on any further discussion (v. 16), all suggest that Paul is not saying what is really on his mind. In ch. 7 he expressed his displeasure with the preoccupation of some at Corinth with such external matters as socio-legal position. Here, on the contrary he fusses about external appearances to such a degree that we are forced to conclude that he sees dress, not as a problem in itself, but as symptomatic of something deeper. Hence, the question is: what is the hidden agenda? To answer this we have to look first at what Paul lays down regarding men and women because only when we have established the meaning of his conclusions can we grasp what his arguments were designed to prove.

Men are forbidden 'to have something hanging down from the head' (v. 4: the RSV is a tendentious paraphrase). This is most naturally understood as a prohibition of 'long hair' in the light of v. 14 which says that men were by nature intended to have short hair. The juxtaposition of v. 15 suggests that it is equally natural for women to have long hair. This in itself suggests that the hidden agenda concerns the differentiation of the sexes. Women should be women, and men should be men, and the difference should be obvious. A fear of homosexuality would be an adequate explanation of Paul's embarrassment when dealing with something that seemed to imply a blurring of sexual distinction. Were all those who protested at the new fashion of long hair for men in our day conscious of the roots of their reaction?

The RSV is very misleading when we try to determine what Paul was saying about women, because it consistently uses 'veil', both as a noun and a verb, where the Greek speaks only of 'a (head) covering'. Paradoxically, where the Greek does use 'veil' (v. 15b), the RSV translates 'covering'. In order to reach Paul's meaning we have to keep in mind the very generic sense of the terms he uses.

In view of what Paul says about men, it is tempting to think that what he criticizes in women is short, mannish hair. This view could claim some support from v. 15, but is decisively contradicted by v. 6. The evidence is not as clear as one might wish, but it seems that at this time well-dressed feminine hair incorporated some form of head-covering, however small. In this perspective, with respect to a woman, 'covered head' would be the equivalent of carefully tended, well-ordered hair, and Paul's objection would be to loose, untidy hair. This fits perfectly with his injunction, 'if a woman cannot, or will not, keep her hair in order, she should cut it off' (v. 6). This is meant only to show his contempt, because he takes it for granted that everyone will agree that it is 'disgraceful for a women to be shorn or shaved' (vv. 6b, 15). The inverse is true for a man. He should have short hair (v. 14). It is a disgrace for him to have a 'covered head', i.e. a feminine hair-do (v. 7a).

At the risk of over-simplification, it seems that what Paul is saying is that women should have feminine hair, and that men should have masculine hair. There is not the slightest hint that he wants to inculcate the subordination of one sex to the other. His concern is distinction not discrimination.

In order to drive home his point that the difference between the sexes should be not only respected but made obvious, Paul uses two lines of argument: the first drawn from the divine intention expressed in creation, and the second drawn from common sense.

The argument from the order of creation appears in v. 3-9, and Paul makes it needlessly complex by using 'head' in two senses, the literal sense and a metaphorical sense meaning 'source or origin' (as we do when we speak of the 'head of the river'). As we might expect, Paul's understanding of the divine intention is drawn from Genesis ch. 2.

Using the metaphorical sense of 'head' Paul begins by saying, 'every man's source is Christ, the source of woman is man, the source of Christ is God' (v. 3). In other words, God is the creator. All other beings owe their origin to him, but in a hierarchical order. Christ, of course, is not mentioned in Genesis, but for believers he was 'the first-born of all creation' (Col 1:15). Thus Christ was involved with God in the creation of man, and all three in the creation of woman. This interpretation is almost as polyvalent as Paul's statement, but the key point is made unambiguously in v. 8-9 which simply repeats Gen 2:18-23. Man was created first, and his rib was used in the creation of woman who was brought into being to be man's helper.

Precisely the same idea appears in v. 7b though expressed more obscurely. Man is the 'image' of God because he exhibited the creativity illustrated in the naming of the beasts (Gen 2:19-20); this act opened a new possibility of being for them. Because he was what God intended him to be, man gave 'glory' to his maker. If woman was created to be man's helper, she gives 'glory' to him, and thus to God, by being what she was intended to be; she honors man by being in reality his complement.

This sort of language obviously tends to make one think that Paul's purpose is to prove the subordination of woman to man. As we have seen, however, this is not his conclusion. Hence, we are forced to deduce that his real argument is the other side of the coin. He is saying in effect, 'If God wanted men and women to be indistinguishable, he would have acted otherwise in the process of creation.'. This interpretation is confirmed by v. 11-12 which explicitly rules out a subordinationist interpretation of Gen 2:18-23.

Paul's second line of argument is based on his contemporaries' sense of the proprieties. He does speak of 'nature itself' (v. 14), but such exaggeration of what is only a widely accepted social custom has been common throughout history. His appeal is to the common-sense assessment that men and women should look different (v. 13-15), and it comes as no surprise to find that this is his personal opinion, and that of the churches he knows (v. 16).

The thrust of Paul's argument, therefore, is that the difference between men and women should be obvious, even though they are equal in terms of their capacity to speak to God in prayer and to declare his word in prophecy. It would be going too far to say absolutely equal, because Paul does introduce a requirement for women which is not applicable to men, 'Therefore, a woman ought to have *authority* on her head, because of the angels' (v. 10). The initial 'therefore' refers to the summary of Gen 2:18-23 in v. 8-9 which had traditionally been used to prove the subordination of woman to man. For Paul this situation had changed, 'therefore' the woman had to have some symbol on her head to show that she now had the 'authority' to fulfil a role previously denied to her (v. 10). This was for the sake of 'the angels' who were associated with the giving of the Law (Gal 3:19) whose application had been modified.

THE LORD'S SUPPER.
11:17-34.

[17]But in the following instructions I do not commend you, because when you come together it is not for the better but for the worse. [18]For, in the first place, when you assemble as a church, I hear that there are divisions among you; and I partly believe it, [19]for there must be factions among you in order that those who are genuine among you may be recognized. [20]When you meet together, it is not the Lord's supper that you eat. [21]For in eating, each one goes ahead with his own meal, and one is hungry and another is drunk. [22]What! Do you not have

houses to eat and drink in? Or do you despise the church of God and humiliate those who have nothing? What shall I say to you? Shall I commend you in this? No, I will not.

[23]For I received from the Lord what I also delivered to you, that the Lord Jesus on the night when he was betrayed took bread, [24]and when he had given thanks, he broke it, and said, "This is my body which is for you. Do this in remembrance of me." [25]In the same way also the cup, after supper, saying, "This cup is the new covenant in my blood. Do this, as often as you drink it, in remembrance of me." [26]For as often as you eat this bread and drink the cup, you proclaim the Lord's death until he comes.

[27]Whoever, therefore, eats the bread or drinks the cup of the Lord in an unworthy manner will be guilty of profaning the body and blood of the Lord. [28]Let a man examine himself, and so eat of the bread and drink of the cup. [29]For any one who eats and drinks without discerning the body eats and drinks judgment upon himself. [30]That is why many of you are weak and ill, and some have died. [31]But if we judged ourselves truly, we should not be judged. [32]But when we are judged by the Lord, we are chastened so that we may not be condemned along with the world.

[33]So then, my brethren, when you come together to eat, wait for one another—[34]if any one is hungry, let him eat at home—lest you come together to be condemned. About the other things I will give directions when I come.

Any slight inclination that Paul might have had to deal tolerantly with hair fashions in the Corinthian community was negated by his awareness that there was something seriously wrong with their liturgical assemblies. 'In giving you this charge (i.e. v. 16) I do not commend you, because when you come together it is not to build up the community but to damage it' (v. 17). It has been reported to him (1:11) that there are divisive factions within the community. These were not the quasi-political groupings (1:12; 3:4) which he has already dealt with (3:5-4:21), but touched the very core of the christian life insofar as they betrayed a lack of concern for the most basic needs of others (v. 21). Paul finds difficulty in giving credence to such a scandalous report, but feels obliged to accept it 'for there must be factions among you in order that those who are genuine among you may be recognized' (v. 19). It is difficult to determine the meaning of 'must' in this verse. Paul certainly does not intend to imply that he is resigned to the inevitability of divisions. Rather he seems to take it for granted that they will occur (for a reason that remains mysterious), and focuses on the positive result, namely, the authentic Christians stand out by their behaviour.

The Lord's supper was intended to be a common meal, a shared repast and Paul's criticism is that the Corinthians made this impossible (v. 20) because no one was concerned about the other (v. 21). Paul's point here is not to condemn gluttony and drunkenness, but to highlight the selfish indifference which is the antithesis of love. It would be better for the Corinthians to eat in their own houses and not to pretend to a unity that their behaviour repudiates. The unity of the church is something more than physical juxtaposition in a determined space. It is a vital sharing of 'life', and the Corinthians cannot deceive themselves that they enjoy this if the physical life of the poor is endangered because they do not have enough to eat. Their behaviour, in addition to humiliating the 'have-nots', shows that they hold true community in contempt (v. 22).

Paul's condemnation of such behaviour is unambiguous, but he could not permit such a situation to continue. He had to remedy it and the approach he takes is an exposition of the eucharist. He tries to convince the Corinthians that their personal involvement with one another in love is necessary for the eucharist to have effective meaning.

He begins by setting down the words used by Jesus to institute the eucharist. These are introduced by the technical terms 'to receive' and 'to deliver' which place Paul as an intermediary in a chain of tradition (v. 23; 15:3). Paul's source is 'the Lord'. Some have interpreted this as meaning that the words of institution were communicated to him in a vision of the Risen Christ, but this hypothesis is rendered unnecessary by the fact that Paul terms the community 'Christ' (6:15; 8:12; 12:12). What he received from the community he received from the Lord. Only thus can we reconcile Paul's statement with the fact that the eucharistic formula betrays the characteristic signs of liturgical usage in a Greek-speaking community. Paul's version of the words of institution (v. 24-25) is most closely related to that of Luke (22:15-20), and it has been plausibly suggested that it records the usage of the church of Antioch which was the base to which Paul returned after each of his missionary journeys.

One feature which sets Paul's version of the eucharistic words apart from all other accounts (Mt 26:26-29; Mk 14:22-25; Lk 22:15-20) is the twice-repeated 'Do this in remembrance of me' (v. 24-25). It is probable that Paul himself added one of these to the traditional formula (compare Lk 22:19) because it is here that we find the link with the factual situation that concerns him. The way in which the Corinthians celebrated the eucharist showed that they 'remembered' Jesus only as a reality of the past. For Paul, on the contrary, authentic remembrance is concerned with the past only insofar as it is constitutive of the present and a summons to the future. What he desires to evoke is the active remembrance of total commitment to Christ which makes the past real in the present, thus releasing a power capable of shaping the future.

The relationship between authentic 'remembrance' and mission is clearly spelled out in the commentary that Paul appends to the liturgical formula (v. 26). The 'proclamation' that he has in mind is neither the symbolic declaration of the death of Jesus in the broken loaf and the outpoured wine, nor the retelling of the Passion during the liturgical celebration. The 'proclamation' takes place in and through the eating of the bread and the drinking of the cup. The material gesture of eating and drinking is not sufficient, as we shall see in v. 27-30. The attitude of the participants is crucial. If their imitation of Christ (11:1) is non-existent or seriously defective, then no matter how carefully the ritual gestures are performed 'it is not the Lord's supper that you eat' (v. 20). Only if the participants have truly put on Christ (Gal 3:27), which is equivalent to putting on love (Col 3:14), is there effective 'proclamation' of the death of Christ in the eucharist. The death of Christ affected the salvation of believers because of the power-laden love it embodied. That same love must continue to be enfleshed in a pattern of behaviour if the death of Christ is to have a permanent saving value. That obligation, which believers assume by becoming members of the Body of Christ, will cease only when it is rendered unnecessary by the physical return of Christ to this world, 'until he comes' (v. 26). Love gave substance to the eucharistic words, and only love can continue to do so.

Having established the authentic 'remembrance' which is demanded of Christians, Paul turns back to the Corinthians and spells out what actually happens when they celebrate the eucharist. 'Whoever, therefore, eats the bread and drinks the cup of the Lord in an unworthy manner will be guilty of the body and blood of the Lord' (v. 27: correct RSV by striking out 'profaning' which does not appear in the Greek). 'To be guilty of the blood of someone' is most naturally understood as meaning 'to be responsible for the death of someone' (Dt. 19:10). The unworthy participant is classed among those who killed Jesus (Heb 6:6; 10:29). Ideally, participation in the eucharist should be a proclamation of the death of the Lord (v. 26) which prolongs its saving love, but the attitude of the participants can make it an act of murder (v. 27).

Obviously, therefore, sharing in the eucharist should be preceded by self-examination (v. 28). This brings us to the crucial question: in such self-examination what criterion or standard should be used? Paul answers, 'Anyone who eats and drinks without discerning the body eats and drinks judgment on himself' (v. 29). The test is 'discernment of the

body'. It is sometimes said that what Paul demands here is
that participants distinguish the eucharist from common
food, but this does not fit the context, and betrays a
preoccupation with the doctrine of the real presence
characteristic of a much later era. Paul's treatment of the
eucharist in fact falls into his beloved A-B-A' pattern:
the situation at Corinth (v. 17-22), the eucharist in itself (v. 23-
26), the situation at Corinth (v. 27-34). The first and third
parts are related as problem and solution. The Corinthians'
acceptance of divisions was a sign to Paul that the 'body'
character of the community (10:17) had not been fully
understood. The 'discernment of the body' which he
demands in v. 29 is the affirmation in action of the organic
unity of the community. Anyone who dares to participate in
the eucharist without adverting to the Body is guilty of
perpetuating the divisions which make the Lord's supper
impossible (v. 20) and, in consequence, eats and drinks to
his own damnation. The Corinthians must sincerely
evaluate their relationship to each other in the light of the
love shown by Christ (2 Cor 5:15) before celebrating the
eucharist (v. 31). In making this demand Paul is merely
restating for a new situation the injunction of Jesus in the
Sermon on the Mount (Mt 5:23-24).

The Corinthians had in fact ignored the demands of
fraternal charity, and Paul goes on to relate this to an
outbreak of illness at Corinth (v. 30). The background here
is the Jewish idea that sin and sickness were intimately
associated (Mk 2:1-12; Jn 9:1-2), and that sickness was a
form of bondage to the powers of evil (Lk 13: 10-17). Having
seriously weakened the unity of the community by their
selfishness, which displayed itself in so many areas (10:20-
21) in addition to the eucharist, it came as no surprise to
Paul that they should be physically afflicted. The protection
of God had been withdrawn in judgment (see on 5:5). But if
the Corinthians recognize that they are being disciplined,
they are offered the opportunity of reforming themselves (v.
32). All they have to do are simple, ordinary things, like
waiting for one another (v. 33), and having a snack before

the liturgical assembly if the pangs of hunger are too sharp (v. 34). They must translate love into such mundane gestures if they are to avoid the condemnation that will fall on the self-centered (v. 32).

The dominant characteristic of Paul's treatment of the eucharist is its extreme realism. There is no exalted poetry, no flight into mysticism. It is firmly rooted in his concept of the community of faith as the basic reality of the New Age introduced by the death of Christ. Christ remains incarnationally present in and to the world through the community that is his Body. The organic unity integral to this Body is reinforced and intensified by the eucharist but not by the words and gestures in themselves, because Paul would energetically repudiate any mechanical approach to the sacrament. Christ is really present only when the words of institution are spoken by 'Christ', an authentic community animated by the creative saving love which alone enables humanity to 'live'. Anything else makes a mockery of Christ's death.

V. 34c shows that there must have been some other problems regarding the liturgical assemblies that the Corinthians had brought to Paul's attention in their letter (see on 7:1). He considers these of minor importance, and decides that they can wait until after his arrival in Corinth (4:19; 16:5-9).

THE GIFTS OF THE SPIRIT.
12:1-11.

12 Now concerning spiritual gifts, brethren, I do not want you to be uninformed. [2]You know that when you were heathen, you were led astray to dumb idols, however you may have been moved. [3]Therefore I want you to understand that no one speaking by the Spirit of God ever says "Jesus be cursed!" and no one can say "Jesus is Lord" except by the Holy Spirit.

[4]Now there are varieties of gifts, but the same Spirit; [5]and there are varieties of service, but the same Lord; [6]and

there are varieties of working, but it is the same God who inspires them all in every one. [7]To each is given the manifestation of the Spirit for the common good. [8]To one is given through the Spirit the utterance of wisdom, and to another the utterance of knowledge according to the same Spirit, [9]to another faith by the same Spirit, to another gifts of healing by the one Spirit, [10]to another the working of miracles, to another prophecy, to another the ability to distinguish between spirits, to another various kinds of tongues, to another the interpretation of tongues. [11]All these are inspired by one and the same Spirit, who apportions to each one individually as he wills.

The opening verse indicates that this topic originated in the Corinthians' letter to Paul (see on 7:1), but the line they took on spiritual gifts and/or the questions they brought up are nowhere clearly stated. Hence, we have to deduce the actual situation at Corinth from what Paul says.

From the way Paul begins (v. 1-3) we can deduce that there was a tendency at Corinth to justify any individual or collective impulse as a motion of the Spirit. The principle of the Strong, for example, 'All things are lawful' (6:12; 10:23), could be drawn into a different domain if those who used it claimed to be under the control of the Spirit. They were 'spiritual men' and every course of action was therefore self-authenticating.

Paul was well aware that the strength of an emotion was no guarantee of its authenticity, and he brings this home to the Corinthians by a reference to their past. 'You know that, while you were still pagans, you were being led away to dumb idols, as if you were carried along' (v. 2). Swept along by the attitude of the society in which they then lived, they had accepted the worship of idols as entirely natural. It had seemed the right thing to do, and this was confirmed by the moments of ecstasy. Paul ironically suggests a contrast between the 'dumb' idols, unable to answer the petitions addressed to them (1 Kgs 18:26-29; Is 46:7), and the noisy uproar of their frenetic worshippers. Since there were many spirit-powers some form of objective criterion is necessary in order to determine what impulses come from the Spirit of God.

As we might expect, this criterion can only be Jesus Christ. He is always the center of Paul's thought. Hence, he lays down that no utterance inspired by the Spirit can be against Jesus, and that every word for Jesus is inspired by the Spirit (v. 3). It is highly significant that Paul here uses 'Jesus' rather than 'Christ', because when he employs 'Jesus' unqualified he normally intends to stress the historicity of the risen Christ. The Corinthians tended to exalt Christ at the expense of Jesus, and to focus on glory rather than on the cross (see on 2:8). It is unlikely that they every said 'Jesus be cursed', but their neglect of the lesson of his historical life (2 Cor 5:15) carried overtones of contempt. Once again, Paul is concerned with the implications of their behaviour (see on 10:14-22), and he formulates a shocking hypothesis to show them where they were heading. On the contrary, anyone who says, either verbally or existentially (see on 11:26), that 'Jesus is Lord' can be sure that their conduct is inspired by the Spirit (Rom 10:9), because they take the historical manifestation of God's love (Rom 8:35, 39) as the model of their obedient service.

Having thus established the fundamental framework within which the impulse of the Spirit must be understood, Paul passes to the individual gifts that the Corinthians have received. The stress of his words suggests that the presence of such gifts within the community had given rise to a competitive spirit. Some gifts appeared more extraordinary than others and singled out the beneficiaries in such a way that they began to assume an air of superiority. Others not so fortunate experienced a feeling of discontent at the quality of their gifts, while still others might have begun to wonder if they had received any gift at all. The situation was ripe for an explosion of envious rivalry.

Hence, Paul has to emphasise that the charismata are 'gifts' bestowed by the Spirit. They are not derived from the natural qualities of individuals. The purpose of such gifts is the 'service' of the Lord. They are not to be used for self-gratification. 'Service', however, is an action which supposes 'power'. The power that is active in them is God 'working' through them. There is no question of any exploitation of their natural resources (v. 4-6). It is not to be expected that each one will receive the same measure of the Spirit. Unity is not a matter of material quantity. It resides ultimately in the one Spirit who gives, the one Lord who is served, and the one God who is at work. Each one, however, has received some gift whose purpose is that all may profit (v. 7; 14:12). 'Common good' (RSV) is an adequate paraphrase, provided that it be understood correctly. The church has no common-good distinct from the individual members of the community, since the community exists to enable each one to be conformed to Christ. The one who knows the needs of the members best is the Spirit who, in consequence, distributes his gifts as he sees fit (v. 11). Those who become conscious of their gift should be on the alert for those who need the service they have been enabled to render.

Paul's point in enumerating various gifts (v. 8-10) is to emphasise that they all come from the same Spirit. The list is illustrative, and is not intended to be comprehensive, as a comparison with similar lists in Paul shows (v. 28; v. 29-30; Rom 12: 6-8; Eph 4:11). All the lists overlap to a certain extent, but each mentions gifts that the others do not. It is possible that different terms are used to designate the same function, but it is impossible to fix precise limits to each gift or even to define them all with anything approximating certitude. In particular, it should never be taken for granted that the conventional definitions current in charismatic groups express Paul's meaning.

THE BODY NEEDS MANY DIFFERENT MEMBERS. 12:12-31.

> [12]For just as the body is one and has many members, and all the members of the body, though many, are one body, so it is with Christ. [13]For by one Spirit we were all

baptized into one body—Jews or Greeks, slaves or free—
and all were made to drink of one Spirit.

14For the body does not consist of one member but of
many. 15If the foot should say, "Because I am not a hand, I
do not belong to the body," that would not make it any
less a part of the body. 16And if the ear should say,
"Because I am not an eye, I do not belong to the body,"
that would not make it any less a part of the body. 17If the
whole body were an eye, where would be the hearing? If
the whole body were an ear, where would be the sense of
smell? 18But as it is, God arranged the organs in the body,
each one of them, as he chose. 19If all were a single organ,
where would the body be? 20As it is, there are many parts,
yet one body. 21The eye cannot say to the hand, "I have no
need of you," nor again the head to the feet, "I have no
need of you." 22On the contrary, the parts of the body
which seem to be weaker are indispensable, 23and those
parts of the body which we think less honorable we invest
with the greater honor, and our unpresentable parts are
treated with greater modesty, 24which our more present-
able parts do not require. But God has so adjusted the
body, giving the greater honor to the inferior part, 25that
there may be no discord in the body, but that the members
may have the same care for one another. 26If one member
suffers, all suffer together; if one member is honored, all
rejoice together.

27Now you are the body of Christ and individually
members of it. 28And God has appointed in the church
first apostles, second prophets, third teachers, then
workers of miracles, then healers, helpers, administrators,
speakers in various kinds of tongues. 29Are all apostles?
Are all prophets? Are all teachers? Do all work miracles?
30Do all possess gifts of healing? Do all speak with
tongues? Do all interpret? 31But earnestly desire the higher
gifts.

And I will show you a still more excellent way.

Paul begins with two simple factual statements, though
these are severely compressed in his formulation. A single

body has many members. The multiplicity of members constitutes a single body (v. 12). The first is a normal way of speaking but gives the impression that the body is somehow distinct from the members it has. The second corrects this by underlining the fact that every part of the body is a member. If we take away all the members there is no body left. This analogy with the physical human body is then applied to 'Christ' (v. 12). As the following verse shows, the christian community is meant (see on 6:15). All, whatever their religious or social origins, were 'baptized into one body' (v. 13). Baptism is a rite of initiation, and even though in one sense it could be said that new converts in virgin mission territory came together in order to constitute a community, it was truer to say that they were joining something that was already in existence. They entered a new environment in which they could breathe the air of freedom which was the gift of the Spirit (Rom 8:2). Since all were now members of the one body and were imbued with the same Spirit, there was no room for the divisions which characterised their past (Col 3:11).

Much has been written regarding the origin of Paul's concept of the community of faith as a 'body', because the idea of 'the body politic' appears in philosophical writings of this period. This, however, is much less important than the sense in which Paul uses 'body'. Is it purely figurative, or does it have a literal meaning? Once it is recognized that, for Paul, the new being of the believer is constituted by love (13:2), there can be no doubt that he intends a very literal meaning. Power is necessary for believers to be released from the enslavement of Sin (= the false value system of the 'world'). Such power is but another name for love (Gal 2:20). To be loved, therefore, is the indispensable prerequisite for authenticity. Individuals become authentically human only when they exercise the creative love which makes them the image of God (11:7; 2 Cor 4:4). One cannot love without loving someone. There is no love that is not focused on a person. The authentic human being, therefore, is necessarily both the object and the source of love. One cannot be as God intended and be alone. To be authentic one must be a vital part in a web of power constituted by the reciprocity of love. The interchange of love is the new being of the believer. Only as part of a greater whole is he 'alive'. The community of faith, therefore, is an organic unity in which each one exists as a dynamic part of the give and take of being. A living organism, such as a plant (Rom 6:5; 11:17-21; Col 2: 6-7; Jn 15: 1-6) or a physical body, is the only natural reality which displays the same characteristics. Hence, when Paul predicates 'body' of the christian community he intends to highlight a fundamental identity. A physical body is exactly the same sort of thing as a community of love. An arm lives only as part of the body. Once amputated it may look the same, but it is dead. Equally, those in 'Christ' are 'alive', whereas those cut off from him (Gal 5:4) are 'dead' (Col 2:13), because the unity of the 'body' consists in a shared life derived from a single vital principle (Col 2:19).

This understanding of the nature of the christian community underlies much that Paul has said in earlier parts of this letter, and it will appear very clearly in chs. 13-14. Here, however, his concern is to show the Corinthians that diversity of spiritual gifts is essential, and he does so very simply and easily by pointing out that without a number of different members a physical body could not exist (v. 14-26). He could have made the same point by referring to a plant. Every organic unity accessible to normal experience demands diversity of parts. A plant is inconceivable without roots, stalk, and leaves. Each part makes a distinct and essential contribution to the being of the whole. The same is true of the diversity within a physical body. A body, all of whose parts are the same, is inconceivable (v. 19).

If the community is a 'body', and if the very being of a 'body' demands a variety of essential contributions, then it follows necessarily that in willing the Body of Christ, God made provision for the required diversity by assigning different gifts to each one (v. 28-31). A community that was all 'administrators' (v. 28) would be as absurd as a body that was all eyes (v. 17).

The way in which Paul formulates his exposition of the need for diversity in organic unity (v. 14-26) inclines commentators to think that, even though he is apparently drawing out an analogy, certain parts should be considered as inspired by the actual situation in Corinth. Thus, v. 15-16 suggest that some members of the community, who had not received remarkable gifts, were inclined to think (or were made to think) that they did not belong to the Body. In the same way, v. 21 suggests that those whose gifts were more brilliant were saying to others that their contributions were unnecessary. The potential for 'discord' (literally 'divisions') is evident (v. 25; 11:18).

This forces Paul to highlight another aspect of the 'body', namely, the cooperation that should obtain among its members. The head cannot do without the feet; the hand does not damage the eye (v. 21). The foot does not kick its own behind. In a 'body' the members care for one another, because if one is injured all suffer, e.g. a headache affects the coordination of hand and eye (v. 25-26). The relevance of this to the situation at Corinth is beyond question. However, it should be noted that even though Paul here insists on coordination and cooperation, this is not the principal point of the analogy between the community of faith and the physical body. Coordination and cooperation are rooted in and made possible by the organic unity of co-existence, i.e. a shared existence in which each one is vitally dependent on the other members.

The section concludes with a series of rhetorical questions (v. 29-30) which Paul intends to be answered in the negative. He is aware, however, that were they seriously posed to the Corinthians their answer would be 'Yes', because all refer to glamour gifts. Hence, he continues (the RSV translation should be changed), 'You strive for (what you believe to be) the higher gifts. I, however, am going to show you a still more excellent way' (v. 31). This is the way of love, which is the supreme gift accorded to everyone.

LOVE THE GREATEST GIFT.
13:1-13.

13 If I speak in the tongues of men and of angels, but have not love, I am a noisy gong or a clanging cymbal. [2]And if I have prophetic powers, and understand all mysteries and all knowledge, and if I have all faith, so as to remove mountains, but have not love, I am nothing. [3]If I give away all I have, and if I deliver my body to be burned, but have not love, I gain nothing.

[4]Love is patient and kind; love is not jealous or boastful; [5]it is not arrogant or rude. Love does not insist on its own way; it is not irritable or resentful; [6]it does not rejoice at wrong, but rejoices in the right. [7]Love bears all things, believes all things, hopes all things, endures all things.

[8]Love never ends; as for prophecies, they will pass away; as for tongues, they will cease; as for knowledge, it will pass away. [9]For our knowledge is imperfect and our prophecy is imperfect; [10]but when the perfect comes, the imperfect will pass away. [11]When I was a child, I spoke like a child, I thought like a child, I reasoned like a child; when I became a man, I gave up childish ways. [12]For now we see in a mirror dimly, but then face to face. Now I know in part; then I shall understand fully, even as I have been fully understood. [13]So faith, hope, love abide, these three; but the greatest of these is love.

The first three statements are all constructed on the same pattern, 'If I have ..., but have not love, I am ...' (v. 1-3). In each case the conditional phrase contains an allusion to one or more of the spiritual gifts mentioned in the previous chapter. Thus, despite its generalizing character, and the fact that it can be lifted out of its context as a complete whole, this chapter has a precise relevance to the situation at Corinth.

In the lists of spiritual gifts in ch. 12 the gift of 'tongues' is always close to the end (v. 10, 28, 30). This was probably intentional because one can easily infer from ch. 14 that the

Corinthians exaggerated the importance of this gift. It was the most unusual and mysterious and so was greatly sought after because it brought its beneficiary into the limelight. Paul had a different hierarchy of values, and 'the tongues of men and even of angels' is mentioned first here because he begins with the gift that contributes least to the community (14:2, 9, 11, 28). Like a gong or cymbal it has a place in an orchestra, but by itself it communicates little, and without love, nothing.

The gifts of prophecy (12:10), knowledge (12:8), and miracle-working faith (12:9) make very real and very important contributions to the community, but without love their beneficiary is 'nothing' (v. 2). This very strong term should not be banalized into a synonym for 'useless'. It means 'non-existent', and this is perfectly comprehensive in Paul's perspective where the new being of the believer is constituted by love. Those who do not love do not exist as God intended them to exist. Thus, when viewed within the perspective of the divine intention for humanity (Rom 8:29), the only standard that Paul recognized, they were 'non-existent'.

The gift of 'helping' (12:28) is dramatized in two actions, rendering oneself destitute to help another, or the acceptance of a supremely painful death in a great cause (v. 3). These come much closer to the type of behaviour that Paul expects of Christians. Nonetheless, they make no contribution to genuine growth if they are not inspired by love. The ideal of christian charity is not to treat others *as if* they were one's best friends, but to *be* to them as life-giving as God is to us in Christ.

This is why Paul defines love in terms of personal attitudes, and not in terms of actions (v. 4-7). Since love is the authentic person (see on v. 2) Paul personifies it, rather than give an abstract definition. He affirms two positive qualities, then denies eight negative qualities, before returning to five positive qualities. This list is obviously not intended to be exhaustive, but neither is it arbitrary. The qualities highlighted reflect the faults manifested by the

Corinthians, or the virtues they neglected. It is instructive to go through the letter and establish the correlations, e.g. 'rejoicing at wrong' is related to the Corinthian attitude towards incest (5:1-8); with regard to idol-meats the Strong were not 'patient and kind' towards the Weak (ch. 8); they 'insisted on their own way', as did the sexual ascetics (ch. 7); and so forth.

In the last paragraph Paul returns to the gifts mentioned in v. 1-3. Thus ch. 13 manifests the A-B-A' pattern, already noted apropos of chs. 12-14 (see introduction to 11:2). If we focus on these gifts we immediately notice a curious narrowing: v. 8 mentions prophecy, tongues, and knowledge; v. 9 evokes only prophecy and knowledge; v. 12 speaks only of knowledge. It seems natural to infer that Paul is especially concerned about 'knowledge'. The object of this 'knowledge' is not expressed, but it is generally understood to be the full vision of God in the life after death. This opinion, however, creates impossible difficulties for the interpretation of v. 13. How can 'faith' remain when full vision has been achieved? How can 'hope' remain when the object desired has been obtained? The only way out of such an impasse is to distinguish different aspects of 'faith' and 'hope', but such mental gymnastics have no support in Paul and are even explicitly contradicted by Rom 8: 24-25 and 2 Cor 5:7.

The whole problem is greatly simplified if we assume that the object of 'knowledge' is the demands of the christian life, and that the 'now' and 'then' (v. 10, 12) contrast the present of the Corinthians with their potential future. At present their insight into what being a Christian really involves is partial (v. 9) and childish (v. 11). The accusation of childishness is made explicitly in 3:1, and enough evidence has been accumulated of the immaturity of the Corinthians. All the things on which they pride themselves Paul has shown to be peripheral to the central concerns of the faith. In the future, however, their awareness can become mature (v. 10) and adult (v. 11) — provided that they heed what Paul is now saying. Growth in love will show them that the ostentatious display in which they now take pride is irrelevant to the essence of christianity which consists in faith, hope, and love (v. 13). Of these three basics love is the most important, because it is the flower of faith and the ground of hope.

PROPHECY MORE IMPORTANT THAN TONGUES. 14:1-25.

14 Make love your aim, and earnestly desire the spiritual gifts, especially that you may prophesy. [2]For one who speaks in a tongue speaks not to men but to God; for no one understands him, but he utters mysteries in the Spirit. [3]On the other hand, he who prophesies speaks to men for their upbuilding and encouragement and consolation. [4]He who speaks in a tongue edifies himself, but he who prophesies edifies the church. [5]Now I want you all to speak in tongues, but even more to prophesy. He who prophesies is greater than he who speaks in tongues, unless some one interprets, so that the church may be edified.

[6]Now, brethren, if I come to you speaking in tongues, how shall I benefit you unless I bring you some revelation or knowledge or prophecy or teaching? [7]If even lifeless instruments, such as the flute or the harp, do not give distinct notes, how will any one know what is played? [8]And if the bugle gives an indistinct sound, who will get ready for battle? [9]So with yourselves; if you in a tongue utter speech that is not intelligible, how will any one know what is said? For you will be speaking into the air. [10]There are doubtless many different languages in the world, and none is without meaning; [11]but if I do not know the meaning of the language, I shall be a foreigner to the speaker and the speaker a foreigner to me. [12]So with yourselves; since you are eager for manifestations of the Spirit, strive to excel in building up the church.

[13]Therefore, he who speaks in a tongue should pray for the power to interpret. [14]For if I pray in a tongue, my spirit

prays but my mind is unfruitful. [15]What am I to do? I will pray·with the spirit and I will pray with the mind also; I will sing with the spirit and I will sing with the mind also. [16]Otherwise, if you bless with the spirit, how can any one in the position of an outsider say the "Amen" to your thanksgiving when he does not know what you are saying? [17]For you may give thanks well enough, but the other man is not edified. [18]I thank God that I speak in tongues more than you all; [19]nevertheless, in church I would rather speak five words with my mind, in order to instruct others, than ten thousand words in a tongue.

[20]Brethren, do not be children in your thinking; be babes in evil, but in thinking be mature. [21]In the law it is written, "By men of strange tongues and by the lips of foreigners will I speak to this people, and even then they will not listen to me, says the Lord." [22]Thus, tongues are a sign not for believers but for unbelievers, while prophecy is not for unbelievers but for believers. [23]If, therefore, the whole church assembles and all speak in tongues, and outsiders or unbelievers enter, will they not say that you are mad? [24]But if all prophesy, and an unbeliever or outsider enters, he is convicted by all, he is called to account by all, [25]the secrets of his heart are disclosed; and so, falling on his face, he will worship God and declare that God is really among you.

Although Paul rightly sees love as the one essential element in the christian life, he cannot ignore the spiritual gifts completely. Since they were given by the Spirit, repudiation was impossible. They had to be integrated into the life of the community. Hence, even though he says, 'Make love your aim', he has to add 'earnestly desire the spiritual gifts' (v. 1) because they were willed by God. In ch. 12 Paul says that such gifts were assigned by God (v. 11) and implies that his choice is not determined by any human qualities of the recipient. This theological truth is here modified by a more practical approach, and Paul's argument rests on the assumption that individuals tend to get the gifts they want. The gift of tongues proliferated at Corinth because the mysterious sound of tongues meant enhanced social prestige. It is difficult to say whether Paul was aware of the possibility of self-deception; it is certainly not excluded by anything he says. His purpose in v. 1-25 is to convince the Corinthians that they should desire to prophesy rather than to speak in tongues. Although presented in a rhetorical declamatory style, his argument is nonetheless carefully articulated.

The criterion by which the relative value of gifts should be judged is their contribution to the building-up of the community (v. 1-5). Tongues have a marked vertical dimension, but their horizontal dimension is nil, because nothing is communicated (v. 2). Tongues can be given a horizontal dimension through the gift of interpretation (v. 5b), but in this case 'spiritual mysteries' (v. 2) are communicated to others, and the combined gifts are virtually indistinguishable from prophecy. Rather than desiring the personal growth (v. 4) which comes from the spiritual soliloquy of tongues, believers should want to prophesy because in this gift the horizontal dimension predominates. It provides the encouragement, edification, and consolation (v. 3) which is indispensable to the spiritual growth of the community.

Paul then develops the thesis that sound without intelligibility contributes nothing to the community (v. 6-12), using three arguments. The first asks what would have happened at Corinth if Paul had come to them speaking in tongues (v. 6). Obviously nothing. He had to be intelligible if he was to be of any use to them. The four activities he mentions—'revelation or knowledge or prophecy or teaching'—all shade too finely into each other for precise definitions to be profitable. The second argument rests on the evident fact that musical instruments communicate something only when their sounds are arranged in an intelligible pattern (v. 7-8). The Corinthians themselves will admit the frustration resulting from musical sounds so unclear that they do not know whether to dance, or weep, or get ready for battle. The third argument evokes the phenomenon of foreign languages (v. 9-12). If I do not speak his language the other is a 'foreigner' (literally 'barbarian'—an onomatopoeic term for unintelligible sounds similar to our 'gibberish'). Yet in the community of faith the other should be a 'brother' (8:11-12)! Hence, the Corinthians should desire to abound in gifts which make a contribution to building-up the church.

Because he accepts that it originates in the Spirit, Paul cannot tell the Corinthians to forget about the gift of tongues completely. All he can do is to try to convince them of the necessity of the gift of interpretation (v. 13-19). He begins by harping on the 'mind' (v. 14-15). It is not involved in the gift of tongues. Since what is said is not framed by the intellect, nothing is communicated to others. The 'mind', therefore, is 'unfruitful'. The force of this argument becomes apparent if we recollect the pride the Corinthians took in the power and sophistication of their intellects (chs. 2 and 8). They prized the 'mind', except in this one instance where unintelligibility gave them social prominence! Were they consistent, they should want to integrate 'mind' and the gift of tongues.

Social prestige accrued to those gifted with tongues because the gift was displayed in public on the occasion of the church's liturgical assemblies. In such assemblies all were supposed to give assent by their 'Amen' to what was uttered (v. 16). This 'Amen' cannot be valid unless all present understand what has been said. Hence, if even one 'outsider', i.e. someone who does not have the gift of interpretation, is present, tongues are out of place (v. 16), because they make a mockery of the responsibility of the church as a whole to test public professions made in its name.

Finally, having dealt with the intra-community aspect of the gift of tongues, Paul turns to its relationship to the apostolate of the community, i.e. its impact on non-believers (v. 20-25). Here he is preoccupied by the witness-value of the community's life. This was so important to him that he begins on a rather acerbic note. 'It is all right to be children in your freedom from malice, but for heaven's sake try to think like adults' (v. 20). Children prefer what glitters and makes a show to what is intrinsically more valuable. The Corinthians manifest the same infantile attitude in their preference for the gift of tongues. In order to bring them up short Paul quotes Is 28:11-12 (v. 21) which was directed to the Israelites who refused to listen to the inspired message of the prophet. He, therefore, threatens them with the terrible gibberish of foreign invaders whom they cannot understand. This forces us to understand 'unbelievers' in v. 22 as a reference to the Corinthians (see on 7:14). They were not 'unbelievers' in the strict sense (see v. 23-24), but a parallel to the unbelieving Israelites is evident. Those who believe, not only in theory but also in practice, give prophecy the importance that is its due (v. 21). Paul does not develop the implicit warning. He wants only to crack the shell of complacency that makes the Corinthians so difficult to reach. Once again (see on 10:1-13) he takes their familiarity with the Jewish scriptures for granted.

Since in Christ they have been given the freedom to acquire authentic humanity, the community has an obligation to non-believers. The quality of its shared existence must be such as to attract outsiders. In order to do this non-believers must see and experience something that excites respect and admiration. However, were an unbelieving outsider to walk into an assembly where all were speaking in tongues, his inevitable reaction would be 'You are raving!' (v. 23), a judgment that would put the christian assembly on the same level as the pagan mystery religions. In this case, the specific character of the community would be totally lost. Believers would be laughed at and despised. A very different impression would be produced if all in the community prophesied (v. 24) because the mutual concern expressed in edification, encouragement, and consolation (v. 3) is so obviously good and so evidently at variance with the self-centeredness of the 'world'. The quality of such a community is a direct challenge to the unbeliever. He is forced to recognize that in such an environment the deepest aspirations of his being can be fulfilled. In consequence, 'he will worship God declaring that God is really among you' (v. 25). This is the effect of genuine witness, a conviction of the *active presence* of God, which is something quite other than the theoretical conviction of the presence of God that is the result of philosophic inquiry (Acts 17:27-28).

ORDER IN THE USE OF SPIRITUAL GIFTS. 14:26-40.

26What then, brethren? When you come together, each one has a hymn, a lesson, a revelation, a tongue, or an interpretation. Let all things be done for edification. 27If any speak in a tongue, let there be only two or at most three, and each in turn; and let one interpret. 28But if there is no one to interpret, let each of them keep silence in church and speak to himself and to God. 29Let two or three prophets speak, and let the others weigh what is said. 30If a revelation is made to another sitting by, let the first be silent. 31For you can all prophesy one by one, so that all may learn and all be encouraged; 32and the spirits of prophets are subject to prophets. 33For God is not a God of confusion but of peace.

As in all the churches of the saints, 34the women should keep silence in the churches. For they are not permitted to speak, but should be subordinate, as even the law says. 35If there is anything they desire to know, let them ask their husbands at home. For it is shameful for a woman to speak in church. 36What! Did the word of God originate with you, or are you the only ones it has reached?

37If any one thinks that he is a prophet, or spiritual, he should acknowledge that what I am writing to you is a command of the Lord. 38If any one does not recognize this, he is not recognized. 39So, my brethren, earnestly desire to prophesy, and do not forbid speaking in tongues; 40but all things should be done decently and in order.

The disedifying turbulence of meetings where all speak in tongues directed Paul's attention to another problem. In a community where so many enjoyed spiritual gifts (v. 26) there could be complete chaos if each one imagined that his gift gave him the right to be heard. This was wrong in principle because 'God is not a God of confusion but of peace (7:15) as in all the churches of the saints' (v. 33), but it was also wrong in practice, because meetings that were either disorderly or too long did not contribute to building-up the community (v. 26). Hence, no matter how many feel impelled, only two or three of those gifted with tongues should be permitted to speak, and then only when there is someone capable of interpreting what they say (v. 27; see on 14:16). Otherwise they must stay silent. Equally, despite the importance that he attaches to prophecy, Paul ordains that only two or three prophets should speak in any given meeting (v. 29). If more were given the floor those listening would be unable to assimilate all that was said, and without this there could be no 'discernment' based on their words. Prophecy is given in order that it be taken to heart. For the same practical reason, no two prophets can speak together. They must take it in turn, and the one speaking must have the humility and generosity to cede the floor if another demands the right to speak (v. 30).

Paul flatly refuses to admit that prophets have no control over their gift, because this is contradicted by the experience of other churches (v. 36). If a thought that could benefit the community flashes into their minds, it can be retained in the memory and brought out when the occasion arises, if not at this particular meeting then at a later one (v. 31-32). Paul obviously expects opposition on this point from the Corinthians. Their childish attitude (14:20) probably led them to exaggerate the dramatic aspects of possession by the Spirit. They delighted in the effect produced when they stood up apparently out of control; the Spirit had chosen *them* as the medium of his message. In order to put a stop to this Paul invokes the full weight of his authority, as he normally does in purely administrative matters. He has been empowered by Christ to direct the community (v. 37; the best Greek manuscripts do not contain the word 'command' here), and if anyone refuses to accept this directive, he is not to be recognized as having a genuine gift of the Spirit (v. 38).

Summing up, Paul underlines that tongues is a real gift. It should not be excluded in principle, but its exercise is subject to the restrictions noted above. Prophecy, however, is to be preferred. But even there the basic criterion is order and decency, because otherwise the community will not be built-up (v. 39-40).

In the above exposition no notice has been taken of v. 34-35 which prohibit women to speak in church. The reason for this is that they were not written by Paul. If these verses are removed no violence is done to his argument. In fact it gains in clarity. Not only are they not integral to this section, but they contradict 11:4, 13 where Paul takes it for granted that women can speak in church and even assume a leadership role. Finally the mention of the Law (presumably the reference is to Gen 3:16) as a decisive argument on a practical issue is totally at odds with Paul's habitual practice. The textual tradition sometimes places v. 34-35 at the very end of this chapter. Hence, they probably originated as a marginal note at a time when social conventions were permitted to limit the freedom of the Spirit.

Part IV.
THE RESURRECTION
15:1-58.

The Resurrection.
15:1-58.

WE HAVE SEEN that a number of problems arose in Corinth because, in opposition to Paul, some in the community believed the body to be morally irrelevant (see on 6:12-20). Following the Greek fashion they considered that the human person was made up of two distinct and separable parts, namely body and soul. The essence of the personality was concentrated in the soul which was immortal, and so it was the attitude of the soul that mattered. The body was a peripheral element destined to corrupt because of its material nature. Corporeal action had no effect on the stance of the soul (6:18b). Some pushed this line to its logical conclusion and denied that there was any resurrection from the dead (15:12). If the body contributed nothing essential in this life, what could be the point of raising it after death?

The only adequate response to this denial is an unwavering affirmation of faith. Paul does in fact provide this, but he goes much further, because the denial was only part of an attack on the incarnational character of christianity. The real point at issue here is the importance of the body, and Paul gives it so much space because he felt that he had to convince the Corinthians that motives and commitment became real only when embodied in a pattern of behaviour modeled on that of Christ. He is fighting for an understanding of the human person as a psychosomatic unity.

THE CREED OF THE CHURCH.
15:1-11.

15 Now I would remind you, brethren, in what terms I preached to you the gospel, which you received, in which you stand, ²by which you are saved, if you hold it fast—unless you believed in vain.

³For I delivered to you as of first importance what I also received, that Christ died for our sins in accordance with the scriptures, ⁴that he was buried, that he was raised on the third day in accordance with the scriptures, ⁵and that he appeared to Cephas, then to the twelve. ⁶Then he appeared to more than five hundred brethren at one time, most of whom are still alive, though some have fallen asleep. ⁷Then he appeared to James, then to all the apostles. ⁸Last of all, as to one untimely born, he appeared also to me. ⁹For I am the least of the apostles, unfit to be called an apostle, because I persecuted the church of God. ¹⁰But by the grace of God I am what I am, and his grace toward me was not in vain. On the contrary, I worked harder than any of them, though it was not I, but the grace of God which is with me. ¹¹Whether then it was I or they, so we preach and so you believed.

Paul begins by reminding the Corinthians of the gospel he preached to them, and of the fact that they had accepted it. This acceptance will save them, provided (a) they live out the gospel in practice, and (b) that Paul told them the truth (v. 1-2).

The second condition is obviously the one that is most important here, and to substantiate it Paul quotes (v. 3b-5) a very early creed originally composed in Aramaic:

Christ died for our sins according to the scriptures
and he was buried
and he was raised on the third day according to the scriptures
and he appeared to Cephas, then to the Twelve.

Much could and should be said about this creed, but in terms of Paul's concern here the two key statements are 'he was buried' and 'he appeared'. The first underlines the reality of Christ's death. Burial put the seal on death as the term of terrestrial human existence (Jgs 8:32; 1 Kgs 2:10; Acts 2:29). The second signifies the return of Christ to the stage of history, and the fact that the creed says 'he appeared to', rather than 'he was seen by' (Gen 2:7), betrays the conviction of the first Christians that something objective came into their experience.

To the witnesses mentioned in the creed Paul adds a series of others (none of whom are mentioned in the gospels) culminating in his own experience on the Damascus road (v. 6-8). It is noteworthy that Paul makes no distinction between the appearance to himself and the appearances to the other witnesses. He takes it for granted that the Jesus who appeared was a real person and not some sort of spirit (Lk 24:36-43). He had not questioned this personally, because we all instinctively trust our own experience, and assumed that it was the same for the others, because they preached exactly what he proclaimed (v. 11).

Christ, therefore, rose from the dead. Nothing is said about the resurrection of anyone else, but we are entitled to assume that the resurrection of all who have died in Christ was part of Paul's preaching (1 Thess 4:16).

CONSEQUENCES OF THE CORINTHIAN THESIS. 15:12-19.

> [12]Now if Christ is preached as raised from the dead, how can some of you say that there is no resurrection of the dead? [13]But if there is no resurrection of the dead, then Christ has not been raised; [14]if Christ has not been raised, then our preaching is in vain and your faith is in vain. [15]We are even found to be misrepresenting God, because we testified of God that he raised Christ, whom he did not raise if it is true that the dead are not raised. [16]For if the dead are not raised, then Christ has not been raised. [17]If

> Christ has not been raised, your faith is futile and you are
> still in your sins. [18]Then those also who have fallen asleep
> in Christ have perished. [19]If for this life only we have
> hoped in Christ, we are of all men most to be pitied.

In order to condition the Corinthians for what he is going
to say later on Paul here shifts his ground. He has to break
down a psychological block, and so he takes the war to the
Corinthians. He says, in effect, 'Let us accept your thesis for
the moment and see what consequences follow from it. If
you find that you cannot accept these logically necessary
inferences, then perhaps you should reconsider your
position.'

If 'there is no resurrection from the dead' (v. 12) these
consequences follow:

   (1) Christ has not been raised (v. 13, 16).
   (2) Paul's preaching is in vain (v. 14), and he is open
       to the accusation of misrepresenting God (v. 15).
   (3) The faith of the Corinthians is meaningless (v.
       14, 17), and they are still in their sins (v. 17).
   (4) Those who died in the hope of resurrection are
       definitively lost (v. 18).

The first conclusion is false (v. 1-11), and this exception
proves the Corinthian thesis to be false. A thesis that does
not cover all the known facts is useless. Some have claimed
that the Corinthians considered the resurrection of Christ a
unique case, but there is no evidence for this. In any case, for
Paul, Christ was truly man (Rom 1:3; 9:5; Gal 4:4), and any
statement covering humanity as a whole had to be
applicable to him. The Corinthians would not be justified in
treating Christ as a special case.

The Corinthians could probably live with the second
conclusion, because Paul had enemies at Corinth. Paul
introduces it only because his preaching was the basis of the
Corinthians' faith. The resurrection was not only an integral
part of his proclamation, it was the keystone of the

theological structure he had communicated to the Corinthians. If they reject the resurrection of Christ the whole edifice falls in ruins, and they are back where they started (n. 3). Obviously it was this point that Paul hoped would touch a nerve at Corinth. If they maintain their position, the distinction between 'those being saved' and 'those perishing' (1:18) is meaningless, and they have no basis for thinking that they possess wisdom or any of the spiritual gifts. They are nothing but ordinary sinners. There is something Machiavellian in the way Paul turns the superiority-complex of the Corinthians (to which he has so frequently objected) against them. The last thing they would want would be to be considered as on the same level as unbelievers, and Paul rubs this in in v. 19. Many pagans held out a vague hope of some change in the human condition, because there was a widespread sense of the futility of contemporary existence. Without the Resurrected Christ, notes Paul, such hope merits only pity, because without Christ the human situation is in fact as hopeless as the phenomenon of death suggests.

CONSEQUENCES OF PAUL'S THESIS.
15:20-28.

> [20]But in fact Christ has been raised from the dead, the first fruits of those who have fallen asleep. [21]For as by a man came death, by a man has come also the resurrection of the dead. [22]For as in Adam all die, so also in Christ shall all be made alive. [23]But each in his own order: Christ the first fruits, then at his coming those who belong to Christ. [24]Then comes the end, when he delivers the kingdom to God the Father after destroying every rule and every authority and power. [25]For he must reign until he has put all his enemies under his feet. [26]The last enemy to be destroyed is death. [27]For God has put all things in subjection under his feet." But when it says, "All things are put in subjection under him," it is plain that he is excepted who put all things under him. [28]When all things are

subjected to him, then the Son himself will also be
subjected to him who put all things under him, that God
may be everything to every one.

Having brandished the stick, Paul now produces the
carrot. Assuming the truth of the resurrection of Christ he
draws out its implications. Human logic has little place here.
It gives way to the passion of the prophet who declares a
conviction that transcends experience and reason.

Since Christ has been raised, it is possible for a man to
return from the realm of the dead. This is now 'known',
whereas before such a return had been only an inference
based on the goodness of God (Dn 12:1-3; 2 Macc 7:9-36).
But if Christ has been raised, he is 'the first-fruits of those
who have fallen asleep' (v. 20). The unstated assumption
here is that Christ had a mission from God to save humanity.
Who he was and what he did were designed to benefit
humanity. His resurrection, therefore, must have implications for all men.

The need for a saviour is spelled out in v. 21-22 which are a
highly condensed statement of Paul's christological anthro-
pology (Rom 5:12-21). Through the sin of Adam the
condition of humanity was changed. Those born after him
were born into a disoriented society whose false value
system they ratified and reinforced by conforming themselves to it. This condemned them to a non-authentic mode
of being which Paul terms 'death', and which culminated in
physical death. A radical change in the human situation was
signalled by the resurrection of Christ because it destroyed
the definitive character of physical death. In and through
Christ men are freed from the false value system of the
'world'. They are no longer 'dead' but 'alive' (Col 2:13). They
now share a mode of being which is not terminated by
physical death. Those who are in Christ (Paul can say 'all'
only in hope) will be made alive eternally.

Paul's thought having moved to the future, he focuses on
the moment when all those in Christ will be raised. This will
be at the Parousia, the Second Coming of Christ (v. 23),

which will bring the world to an end. The reason for the interval between the resurrection of Christ and the general resurrection of those who belong to him through faith and baptism is the fact that Christ's mission was not complete at his death. 'He must reign until he has put all his enemies under his feet' (v. 25). Having been exalted to the position of Lord through his resurrection (Rom 1:3-4; 14:9; 1 Cor 15:45), Christ still had to annihilate the hostile powers who still held the great mass of humanity in subjection to a false value system. At his death the power of forces hostile to authentic human development had been broken, but they had not been definitively crushed (see on 10:14-22). The evil influences operative in the 'world' act on those who are physically alive, and so these must be destroyed first (v. 24), but Death is the master of those who have died, and so his turn necessarily comes next (v. 26).

When this definitive victory has been won, when the words of Ps 8:7 (referring to mankind before the fall) and Ps 110:1 (referring to the Messiah) have been fulfilled, then Christ will present his kingdom to God (v. 24), and he will remit into God's hands the authority given him for his mission (v. 28). The subordination of Christ, precisely as 'Son', to God could not be expressed with greater clarity, and is in total accord with the stress on his humanity in v. 21.

AD HOMINEM ARGUMENTS FOR THE RESURRECTION.
15:29-34.

[29]Otherwise, what do people mean by being baptized on behalf of the dead? If the dead are not raised at all, why are people baptized on their behalf? [30]Why am I in peril every hour? [31]I protest, brethren, by my pride in you which I have in Christ Jesus our Lord, I die every day! [32]What do I gain if, humanly speaking, I fought with beasts at Ephesus? If the dead are not raised, "Let us eat and drink, for tomorrow we die." [33]Do not be deceived: "Bad company ruins good morals." [34]Come to your right mind,

and sin no more. For some have no knowledge of God. I say this is to your shame.

'Baptism for the dead' when taken in isolation lends itself to many different interpretations. The probable meaning, however, is that demanded by the immediate context. In vv. 31-32 Paul gives an example of the type of suffering that his vocation imposed. V. 30 is an evident transition from the 3rd. per. pl. in v. 29 to 1st. per. sing. of v. 31, because it is in 1st. per. pl. (correct RSV). Thus, v. 29 appears as a general statement which is then clarified by a particular example; it must therefore concern the sufferings associated with his apostolic labors. Now we can see the connection with v. 28. The Son has been entrusted with a specific mission to whose exigencies he is subjected until it is accomplished. The parallel with his own situation (cf. 15:8-10) suggested a new argument for the resurrection based on his own experience, viz. the strength of his belief as witnessed by his sufferings.

The spiritual elite at Corinth had mocked Paul and his co-workers by saying that they were 'destroying themselves for the sake of those dead to the higher spiritual truths'; one of the meanings of *baptizein* is 'to destroy, perish'. They saw his dedication but considered his efforts misdirected. Paul saw the fact as common-ground on which to base an argument, and to this end intensified their interpretation. He was working not only for those who were 'dead' in an existential sense, but for those who had died (15:18) or would die; thus v. 29b must be translated (correct RSV): "If those who are *really* dead are not raised, why do some work themselves to death on their behalf?" The question is not answered directly, but the response is implicit in what Paul goes on to say regarding his sufferings. Only a deeply rooted belief in the resurrection could make him continue to place himself in continuous danger (v. 30). This general statement is then reinforced by a particular example (v. 32a). Since Roman citizens could not be condemned to the arena without first being deprived of their citizenship, and Paul still possessed his much later (Acts 22:25-29), 'fighting with beasts' must be understood as a metaphorical reference to a situation of grave danger (Ps 22:12-16; 2 Tim 4:17) arising from opposition at Ephesus (16:8; Acts 18:19-21; 19:1-12).

Were Paul not driven by a radical conviction concerning the resurrection, he would have acted very differently. If death is the end the sensible reaction is to make the most of the pleasures of the passing moment (v. 32b). The quotation from Is 22:13 was widely echoed throughout the Greco-Roman world. For example, a tombstone was inscribed with the words, 'Drink—for you see the end'. Not all who deny the resurrection draw this conclusion, but it would be reasonable to do so. And Paul underlines that it is likely that many will in fact do so by means of a quotation from Menander's lost comedy *Thais* (v. 33). Unless extreme care is taken the ideas of a fallen 'world' can penetrate into the christian community and destroy its freedom. The force of Paul's argument here is that it brackets the Corinthians with the unbelievers whom they held in contempt (see on 6:4 and 10:17).

Paul concludes the series of ad hominem arguments with a very sharp admonition where the key verb means to sleep off a bout of drunkeness, 'Wake up properly to a sober life, and stop sinning' (v. 34). Those who denied the resurrection probably thought of themselves as sober thinkers who knew the truth about God, and who condemned belief in the resurrection as the fantasy of those drunk with enthusiasm. The force of the series of arguments was to class them among those who have 'no knowledge of God', and this, for Paul, is a matter of shame, because his whole work among them had been dedicated to the inculcation of the revelation that God had given in Christ. Without Christ (and from Paul's point of view to deny the resurrection was to deny the Christ he preached) there is only sin and spurious knowledge.

THE RESURRECTED BODY.
15:35-49.

35But some one will ask, "How are the dead raised? With what kind of body do they come?" 36You foolish man! What you sow does not come to life unless it dies. 37And what you sow is not the body which is to be, but a bare kernel, perhaps of wheat or of some other grain. 38But God gives it a body as he has chosen, and to each kind of seed its own body. 39For not all flesh is alike, but there is one kind for men, another for animals, another for birds, and another for fish. 40There are celestial bodies and there are terrestrial bodies; but the glory of the celestial is one, and the glory of the terrestrial is another. 41There is one glory of the sun, and another glory of the moon, and another glory of the stars; for star differs from star in glory.

42So is it with the resurrection of the dead. What is sown is perishable, what is raised is imperishable. 43It is sown in dishonor, it is raised in glory. It is sown in weakness, it is raised in power. 44It is sown a physical body, it is raised a spiritual body. If there is a physical body, there is also a spiritual body. 45Thus it is written, "The first man Adam became a living being"; the last Adam became a life-giving spirit. 46But it is not the spiritual which is first but the physical, and then the spiritual. 47The first man was from the earth, a man of dust; the second man is from heaven. 48As was the man of dust, so are those who are of the dust; and as is the man of heaven, so are those who are of heaven. 49Just as we have borne the image of the man of dust, we shall also bear the image of the man of heaven.

Once again the tone changes. The situation here is the reverse of that in v. 12-19. There Paul assumed the Corinthian position and showed it to be wrong by demonstrating that it led to unacceptable conclusions. Here an objector does the same thing to Paul, saying in effect, 'Let us suppose the dead are raised. Then, they must have bodies. But we have not the faintest idea of what such bodies will be like. Therefore, it is pointless to continue the discussion.' (v. 35). In essence Paul's response is to show that it is possible to make a reasonable estimate of what the resurrection body will be like, and that this estimate is verified in the resurrection body of Christ.

Paul begins by reminding his questioner of the phenomenon of plant life. A seed has one type of body which is lost when it is buried in the earth. The plant that emerges is the same being but it has a radically different body (v. 36-37). The form of the plant-body is determined by God, and no one could guess his intention from the form of the seed-body, particularly since so many different plants come from seeds that look very much alike (v. 38).

Paul then develops this last point by showing that words like 'flesh', 'body' and 'glory' are not univocal terms. There are many different kinds of 'flesh' (v. 39), many different kinds of 'body' (v. 40a), and many different kinds of 'glory' (v. 40b-41). What Paul is trying to convey here is that the realities to which we apply these terms may not be the only realities to which such terms can be applied.

Having opened the mind of his questioner Paul is now in a position to deal directly with the resurrection body (v. 42-44a). The verbs used imply a 'before' and 'after' which refer to the present and future life respectively. The verb 'sow' is important because it applies the idea developed in v. 36-38, namely, that continuity may be accompanied by radical change. The qualities of the two states may be tabulated thus:

Present Body	*Resurrection Body*
Perishable	Imperishable
Dishonor	Glory
Weakness	Power
Physical	Spiritual

The resurrection body is obviously a mirror image of the present body — everything is reversed. The qualities which make the present body a burden in this life are simply negated and replaced by their opposites. The size and composition of the present body impose obvious limitations; there are places it cannot go, things it cannot do. It is susceptible to attack by various forms of illness, and of itself it tends to corrupt. 'Dishonor' would be better rendered by 'inglorious', because Paul simply wanted an antithesis to 'glory'. 'Glory' in this sense means 'righteousness-in-splendour'. Adam and Eve enjoyed this quality before the Fall (*Apocalypse of Moses* 20:1-2; 21:5-6), but lost it for themselves and for all others through their sin (v. 21; Rom 3:23). Such 'glory' (like 'life'; see on v. 21-22) is inchoatively possessed already by those who are in Christ (2 Cor 3:18), and will come to full brilliance in the resurrection body (Dn 12:3), which will in addition be incorruptible, powerful, and spiritual.

Paul then anticipates the obvious objection, namely, such a resurrection body may be conceivable, but is there any reason to think that it is anything more than a pure possibility? In other words, how do we know that it is not merely an example of wishful thinking? He replies, 'If there is a physical body, there is also a spiritual body' (v. 44b). Paul, as we might expect, is thinking of the Risen Christ, but in order to understand his presentation (v. 45-49) the background must be filled in a little.

In dealing with 2:6-3:4 we saw that the Corinthians were influenced by a type of hellenized Jewish speculation of which the best known representative is Philo. On the basis of the two accounts of the creation of man in Genesis, Philo discerned two Adams, the first made 'in the image of God' (Gen 1:27), the second made 'of dust from the ground' and endowed with a 'living soul' (Gen 2:7; quoted in v. 45). The first was the archetypal man, humanity as God desired it to be; the second was humanity as it actually was. It was a common Jewish belief that there was a correspondence between the Beginning and the End. Thus, there would be a Last Adam who enjoyed all the qualities of the First Adam of Gen 1:27, and who would be the antithesis of man as he actually is.

Paul takes up the basic element of this belief, the two Adams, but (exactly as in 2:6-3:4) gives the key terms a different meaning. This he can do because for him Christ was the perfect embodiment of humanity as God intended it. According to Philo the 'spiritual' Adam came first, and then the 'physical' (from *psyche* = 'soul'; Gen 2:7) Adam. Aware that Genesis contains two accounts of *the same event*, Paul says simply that both these Adams are 'physical', and that the 'spiritual' Adam must be sought elsewhere (v. 46-47). The true Adam is the Last Adam who is Christ. The Corinthians had accepted Christ as 'a life-giving spirit' (v. 45b); their conversion to Christ was the basis of what they conceived as their spirit-filled existence. They tended to pass over in silence the earthly existence of Christ and in particular his crucifixion (see on 2:8 and 12:3), but this does not bother Paul here, because what he said in v. 1-19 shows that the Christ who is 'a life-giving spirit' is the resurrected Christ (suggested here by 'became'). The resurrection body of Christ, therefore, shows the reality of the portrait of the resurrection body drawn in v. 42-44a. The Corinthians had experienced the 'power' of Christ and they confessed him as 'the Lord of glory' (2:8). Hence, Paul can confidently state, 'Just as we have borne the image of the man of dust (i.e. the strain in our physical being derived from the fallen Adam which means that we shall die), we shall also bear the image of the man of heaven (i.e. we shall enjoy a resurrection body like that of Christ)' (v. 49).

THE NEED FOR TRANSFORMATION.
15:50-58.

> 50I tell you this, brethren: flesh and blood cannot inherit the kingdom of God, nor does the perishable inherit the imperishable.
> 51Lo! I tell you a mystery. We shall not all sleep, but we shall all be changed, 52in a moment, in the twinkling of an eye, at the last trumpet. For the trumpet will sound, and the dead will be raised imperishable, and we shall be changed. 53For this perishable nature must put on the

imperishable, and this mortal nature must put on immortality. [54]When the perishable puts on the imperishable, and the mortal puts on immortality, then shall come to pass the saying that is written:

"Death is swallowed up in victory."

[55]O death, where is thy victory?

O death, where is thy sting?"

[56]The sting of death is sin, and the power of sin is the law. [57]But thanks be to God, who gives us the victory through our Lord Jesus Christ.

[58]Therefore, my beloved brethren, be steadfast, immovable, always abounding in the work of the Lord, knowing that in the Lord your labor is not in vain.

Having shown that it is possible to conceive of a resurrection body, and that Christ in fact possesses such a body, Paul now underlines that a body other than that which we now enjoy is necessary for the new type of existence that will follow death. He has to deal with two cases, those who have already died and those who survive to see the Parousia.

In Paul's language the distinction is between 'flesh and blood', a Semitic formula applied only to living persons (Mt 16:17), and 'corruption' (not 'perishable'), i.e. corpses in the process of decomposition (v. 50). Something that lends itself to decomposition is incompatible with a mode of being that endures eternally ('incorruption', not 'imperishable'). This is obviously true of the dead, but it is equally true of those who are still alive. These may not 'die' in the same way, but a transformation of their bodies is nonetheless necessary (v. 51), because it was by accident that they were alive at the Parousia. Otherwise, they would have died and decomposed. Hence, what is 'perishable' and 'mortal' must be made imperishable and immortal in order to endure eternally (v. 53).

The statement 'we shall not all sleep' (v. 51; v. 18) betrays Paul's conviction that the Second Coming of Christ was imminent (1 Thess 4:15). The sound of the trumpet of God will awake the dead (1 Thess 4:16). The imagery is identical with that of 1 Thess, but the denial of the resurrection and/or the objections raised against it forced Paul's thought to develop. In 1 Thess he is rather vague, 'we who are alive, who are left shall be caught up together with them (the dead) in the clouds to meet the Lord in the air, and so we shall always be with the Lord' (4:17). Here, he has become conscious of the need for a new type of body adapted to this new mode of existence (v. 52-53).

The Parousia, therefore, will be the great moment when Death is finally and definitively vanquished (v. 54-55; quoting Hos 13:14). The mention of Death distracts Paul for a second, because he is accustomed to link Death, Sin, and Law (v. 56). Sin, here is the false-value system of the 'world'. Forcing itself on individuals it leads to the mode of being called 'death' which leads to physical death. One aspect of this false-value system was that it exaggerated the role and importance of the Law. Sin exercised its power by forcing individuals to give blind obedience to the Law, thereby depriving them of the freedom to decide, which is the basis of authenticity. In Christ the believers have already been freed from Sin and the Law (Rom 6:17-18; 7:7). They have been freed from 'death' (Col 2:13), but at the Parousia they are freed from Death in its most radical form. Quite naturally Paul bursts out in thanksgiving, because this victory is possible only because God is acting through Christ (v. 57).

Paul concludes with an admonition (v. 58). His long argument has been motivated by love, because unless the Corinthians remain 'steadfast and immovable' in the resurrection faith that he handed on to them (v. 1-6) they will not participate in the victory of which he has just spoken. To remain true to this faith will not be easy, but they will find the effort well worthwhile.

Part V.
LAST WORDS.
16:1-24.

Last Words.
16:1-24.

AS IS USUAL with Paul the last portion of a letter is a mixture of information, exhortation, and greetings. Here Paul becomes truly personal. He talks about his plans, mentions friends who are with him, greets friends that he has not seen for some time. No big theological problems are introduced, and we are permitted to catch a glimpse of the everyday life of the communities of the first century, and to see something of the web of human contacts which enabled them to grow together.

THE COLLECTION FOR JERUSALEM.
16:1-4.

> **16** Now concerning the contribution for the saints: as I directed the churches of Galatia, so you also are to do. [2]On the first day of every week, each of you is to put something aside and store it up, as he may prosper, so that contributions need not be made when I come. [3]And when I arrive, I will send those whom you accredit by letter to carry your gift to Jerusalem. [4]If it seems advisable that I should go also, they will accompany me.

The opening words suggest that the Corinthians had heard of Paul's project to relieve the poor of Jerusalem (Gal 2:10), and so inquired as to how this collection was to be organized (see on 7:1). This collection was a big undertaking

(Acts 11:30; 24:17; Rom 15:25-28; 2 Cor 8-9), and while it was important to Paul insofar as it was a concrete symbol of the unity of the different churches, it was not his highest priority. Hence he orders that the most time-consuming part should be out of the way by the time he arrives. On the first day of the week, Sunday, each member is to put by whatever can be spared, so that when Paul comes each will have a sum of money ready to be paid into a central fund (v. 2). There is no question of paying into a central fund each week, possibly because Paul was afraid of the trouble that would result if some of the money was thought to have gone astray. That Paul was conscious of this aspect is clear in vv. 3-4 which can only be interpreted as manifesting Paul's desire to have everyone know that his hands were perfectly clean (see on 9:1-18). Those who carry the money to Jerusalem will be accredited by Paul, but they must be selected by the community, and Paul himself will accompany them, only if the community deems it advisable. Since it is a question of practical administration Paul is dogmatic in deciding what should be done.

PAUL'S TRAVEL PLANS.
16:5-9.

> [5]I will visit you after passing through Macedo'nia, [6]and perhaps I will stay with you or even spend the winter, so that you may speed me on my journey, wherever I go. [7]For I do not want to see you now just in passing; I hope to spend some time with you, if the Lord permits. [8]But I will stay in Ephesus until Pentecost, [9]for a wide door for effective work has opened to me, and there are many adversaries.

Paul's mention of a visit to Corinth (v. 3) leads him to a fuller account of his plans for the future. He is at present in Ephesus, and feels it necessary to stay there until Pentecost (v. 8) because, while there are many eager converts, there are many who tenaciously attempt to impede his activity. Paul feels that the community would be at risk without the reinforcement of his presence. However, he cannot permit the Ephesians to cling to his coat-tails forever, and in a couple of months he feels that he will have brought them to the point where they can survive without him.

Then he plans to make a swing through Macedonia (v. 5). During his second missionary journey (49-52 AD) he had founded communities there that he had not seen for over five years. He had written to the Thessalonians and the Philippians, but these communities did not pose anything like the problems that had arisen at Corinth. Hence, he was going to 'pass through' Macedonia (v. 5), but counted on 'staying' at Corinth (v. 6). He does not want to come to Corinth immediately (v. 7), perhaps because there was some minor problem in Macedonia which he felt demanded his attention, but more likely because the Corinthians might send him to Jerusalem (v. 4). In that case he would not get to Macedonia in the foreseeable future. Paul does not fix the duration of his stay at Corinth. The complexity of the problem touched on in this letter reveals that he could expect a difficult time. If he had not succeeded in restoring peace, order, and sanity by the end of the summer he would have to stay throughout the winter. Snow in the high country made an overland journey to Jerusalem virtually impossible, and ships going east at that season were rare because the seas were dangerous (Acts 27:9-10). These plans did not work out exactly as Paul planned (Acts 19:21-20:3), and he had to placate the Corinthians who accused him of misleading them (2 Cor 1:15-24; 2:12-13).

VARIOUS BRETHREN.
16:10-18.

> [10]When Timothy comes, see that you put him at ease among you, for he is doing the work of the Lord, as I am. [11]So let no one despise him. Speed him on his way in peace, that he may return to me; for I am expecting him with the brethren.
>
> [12]As for our brother Apol′los, I strongly urged him to visit you with the other brethren, but it was not at all his

will to come now. He will come when he has opportunity.
¹³Be watchful, stand firm in your faith, be courageous,
be strong. ¹⁴Let all that you do be done in love.

¹⁵Now, brethren, you know that the household of
Steph'anas were the first converts in Acha'ia, and they
have devoted themselves to the service of the saints; ¹⁶I
urge you to be subject to such men and to every fellow
worker and laborer. ¹⁷I rejoice at the coming of Steph'anas
and Fortuna'tus and Acha'icus, because they have made
up for your absence; ¹⁸for they refreshed my spirit as well
as yours. Give recognition to such men.

Timothy's going to Corinth has already been mentioned
(4:17). Here there seems to be some doubt because the Greek
has '*if* he comes' (v. 10). It may be that Timothy had been
sent to Macedonia (Acts 19:22) with the option of going on
to Corinth if he got instructions, which could easily fail to
reach him. The grim reality of the apostolic life is
highlighted by Paul's anxiety that his young colleague
should be made to feel at home, and in particular that no one
should look down on him (v. 10b-11). The Corinthian
Christians could be exceedingly disagreeable (see 2 Cor
10:10; 11:6-7; 29; 12:11-21) and needed little provocation.

The sophisticated eloquence of Apollos (Acts 18:24-28),
on the contrary, had won him a large following at Corinth
(1:11; 3:4) who took exception to the fact that he had not
visited them for some time. Perhaps in their letter they had
accused Paul of hindering his rival! Something like this is
necessary to justify Paul's earnest explanation that he had
tried to persuade Apollos to go, and that it was the latter
who refused (v. 12; the RSV reference to the will of 'God' is
not certain).

Much of what has been read in this letter suggests that the
church at Corinth was entirely composed of rather weird
individuals. It would be natural, however, to suspect that
there were exceptions, and such in fact proves to be the case.
Paul's first converts at Corinth (he says 'Achaia' but see Acts
17:34) were the members of the household of Stephanas, and

these turned out to be exactly the sort of Christians that Paul desired. Becoming aware of a need 'they appointed themselves for the service of the saints' (v. 15). Their concern was not for themselves but for others. There is a faint hint that this group played an authoritative role, but we can say nothing more. Perhaps they tried to act as mediators between the various factions. In any case, Paul calls on the Corinthians to recognize their ministry, as he does (v. 16). The 'submission' that he desires to be given to them, and to others who might make the same contribution, is not obedience to dictates, but acceptance of the challenge of the quality of their christian lives. It must be presumed that the household of Stephanas included women.

Information concerning this household must have been brought by its head who is mentioned, with Fortunatus and Achaicus, as having come from Corinth (v. 17). They may have been the bearers of the letter (see on 7:1) to which Paul devotes so much space in this epistle. In which case, Paul must have been trying very hard to be nice in saying 'they have made up for your absence'. Good company as they were, the news they brought was anything but 'refreshing'! The Corinthians should 'give close attention' to such Christians.

FINAL GREETINGS.
16:19-24.

> ¹⁹The churches of Asia send greetings. Aquila and Prisca, together with the church in their house, send you hearty greetings in the Lord. ²⁰All the brethren send greetings. Greet one another with a holy kiss.
> ²¹I, Paul, write this greeting with my own hand. ²²If any one has no love for the Lord, let him be accursed. Our Lord, come! ²³The grace of the Lord Jesus be with you. ²⁴My love be with you all in Christ Jesus. Amen.

Trying to forge links between widely separated communities was one of Paul's preoccupations, and he loses no opportunity to greet one in the name of the others. Aquila and Prisca came to Corinth as Jewish refugees from Rome. Paul met them there, and because they had the same trade, he lived and worked with them (Acts 18:1-3). Why and when they moved to Ephesus is not known. They would have been known to the Corinthians, and Paul may even have been staying with them. Later they moved back to Rome (Rom 16:3). Their journeys, and the fact that they had a house big enough to host a local community of the Ephesian church, suggest that they were wealthy.

'Greet one with a holy kiss' (v. 20b). Paul's letters were probably read in the public assembly of the community, and so at the end he asks them to give one another the salutation which he would have given had he himself been present (Rom 16:16).

The last paragraph is written in Paul's own hand (v. 21), indicating very clearly that the rest of the letter was written by someone else. Paul must have used a secretary, as he did in the letter to the Romans (Rom 16:22). A trained scribe could write much more quickly and neatly than Paul could (Gal 6:11), but this opened the door to forgery (2 Thess 2:2), and so Paul made a practice of authenticating his letters (2 Thess 3:17; Gal 6:11; Col 4:18; Philem 19).

Prior to the final blessing (v. 23-24) Paul abruptly introduces two phrases 'If anyone does not love the Lord, let him be anathema' and the Aramaic *Marana tha*, which were probably part of the liturgy. They are an effective reminder to the Corinthians that the ultimate test of discipleship is the active recognition of love that Jesus is Lord (12:3), and that they must live in the vigilant expectation of his return in glory. Paul's last word to those who gave him so much trouble is 'love'.

FOR FURTHER READING

C. K. Barrett, *A Commentary on the First Epistle to the Corinthians* (Black's New Testament Commentaries), London: Black, 1968; reprinted in paperback 1971.
> Should be read by anyone seriously interested in 1 Corinthians. Written with extraordinary clarity and perception. All the problems of the letter are discussed in detail but in such a way that the enthusiasm of the non-specialist is not blunted.

W. F. Orr and J. A. Walther, *I Corinthians* (Anchor Bible), Garden City, NY: Doubleday, 1976.
> Though the commentary avoids many of the real problems of the letter it is prefaced by a useful biography of Paul.

J. Ruef, *Paul's First Letter to Corinth* (Pelican New Testament Commentaries), London: Penguin, 1971.
> A rather dull and heavy verse-by-verse explanation, but some good insights.

J. Murphy-O'Connor, O.P., *Becoming Human Together*, Glazier/Veritas: Wilmington/Dublin, 1977.
> A simple exposition of Paul's understanding of the humanity of Christ, and of the structures of inauthentic existence (Sin, Law, Death, Isolation) and of authentic existence (Freedom, Community). Provides a systematic framework in which 1 Corinthians can be read with greater profit.

J. Blenkinsop, *The Corinthian Mirror* (Stagbook), Sheed and Ward: London/New York, 1964.
> Highlights aspects of 1 Corinthians which have special relevance to the contemporary situation of the church.

Jerusalem Bible, Garden City, NY/London: Doubleday/Longman, Darton, Todd, 1966.
> Translation not always accurate, but notes and marginal references of the full edition are invaluable.

Bibliography

For those who might be interested, the points on which my commentary differs from the current consensus are documented in a series of articles which I have published.

"1 Corinthians 5:3-5."
Revue Biblique 84 (1977) 239-45.

"Corinthian Slogans in 1 Cor 6:12-20."
Catholic Biblical Quarterly 40 (1978) 391-96.

"The Divorced Woman in 1 Cor 7:10-11."
Journal of Biblical Literature 100 (1981)

"Faith without Works in 1 Cor 7:14."
Revue Biblique 84 (1977) 349-61.

"Freedom or the Ghetto (1 Cor 8:1-13; 10:23-11:1)."
Revue Biblique 85 (1978) 543-74.

"1 Cor 8:6 — Cosmology or Soteriology?"
Revue Biblique 85 (1978) 253-67.

"Food and Spiritual Gifts in 1 Cor 8:8."
Catholic Biblical Quarterly 41 (1979) 292-98.

"The Non-Pauline Character of 1 Cor 11:2-16?"
Journal of Biblical Literature 95 (1976) 615-21.

"Sex and Logic in 1 Cor 11:2-16."
Catholic Biblical Quarterly 42 (1980) 482-500.

"Eucharist and Community in 1 Cor."
Worship 50 (1976) 370-85; 51 (1977) 56-69.

"Tradition and Redaction in 1 Cor 15:3-7."
Catholic Biblical Quarterly 43 (1981) 582-89.

"'Baptized for the Dead' (1 Cor 15:29) — A Corinthian Slogan?"
Revue Biblique 88 (1981)